UNIQUE YOU

PRACTICAL STEPS TO DISCOVER AND LIVE YOUR LIFE'S PURPOSE

this page Intentionally left blank

UNIQUE YOU

PRACTICAL STEPS TO DISCOVER AND LIVE YOUR LIFE'S PURPOSE

CYNTHIA ARKU, Ph.D.

Shidaanikei
TORONTO

Shidaanikei Publishers Incorporated

Incorporated in Canada www.shidaanikei.com

Cover design by Shidaanikei Graphic Design Department

Library and Archives Canada Cataloguing in Publication

Title: Unique you: practical steps to discover and live your life's purpose /Dr. Cynthia Arku. Names: Arku, Cynthia, author. Identifiers: Canadiana 20210395613 | ISBN 9781990604041 (softcover) Subjects: LCSH: Self-actualization (Psychology)—Religious aspects—Christianity. | LCSH: Self-realization—Religious aspects—Christianity. | LCSH: Conduct of life. | LCSH: Christian life. Classification: LCC BV4598.2 .A75 2022 | DDC 248.4—dc23

PRINTED AND BOUND IN CANADA, 2022

Praises for "Unique You"

"This book is like a buffet menu. There's something for everyone, young and old, beginner and experienced in life, professionally stable and searching out, married and unmarried, religious, and non-religious and so on. It makes a strong case that finding one's purpose in life is an inside job of discovering what you're made of and made for. The Bible admonishes every person to "know him/herself."

Unfortunately, confusion, ignorance, upbringing, associations, innocuous and blatant personal mistakes may distract or result in loss of God's intended purpose for an individual's life. The author is convincingly emphatic that transformation is possible regardless of an individual's state and stage on this life's course.

It begins with connecting with God the purpose Giver and aligning with the right mix of imagination, mentors and mentees, relationships, resources, and decision-making strategies. This connection and alignment will empower you to successfully achieve your purpose. I recommend this book for families, learning institutions and professional bodies."

Dr. Kenneth O. Mensah
London, Ontario, Canada.

"I believe this book will impart wisdom on whoever reads it. This book has outlined some issues that are common to most people and has applied the knowledge from God's word to help solve those issues."

Greg S.
Edmonton, Alberta, Canada

"They say that experience is the greatest teacher. This book clearly shows that Dr. Cynthia Arku has a well-rounded knowledge of life and its complexities. She has even ventured to outline some solutions to life's problems. Informative and enlightening! Well-suited for this modern-day generation.

As Dr. Arku rightly states: "God hard-wired you (us) so that we won't be a disappointment to Him (God), humanity and yourself." In conclusion, I dare quote from

Proverbs 8: 10 -11 "Choose my instruction instead of silver, knowledge rather than choice gold, for wisdom is more precious than rubies, and nothing you desire can compare with her."

Janette Edwards
Edmonton, Alberta, Canada

"This book is very insightful. Really, what not to follow or get into, is just as important as what or who to consult and observe. We decided our grandchildren or children could really benefit from these insights. This guide illustrates the need to walk closely with God, and to hear His voice about our choices early in life. Also, it is always possible at any age, to align ourselves with God's purposes for our life. Cynthia has beautifully illustrated ways to do this! We highly recommend this book for the young and old. Enjoy!"

Robert and Judith Laybourne
Okotoks, Alberta, Canada.

"This book is thought-provoking and rich in details that will shape who you're as a person. If you're at a crossroads, a beginner or mature, there is something for you in this book. I suggest that you read it to guide you on your next path forward to a life filled with purpose, blessings, and opportunities. It is a great read and a future bestseller!"

Monica Ansah-Sam, P. Eng. – Ontario, Canada.

"I am truly touched, challenged, intrigued, and encouraged. This book speaks to people of all ages and in many situations, circumstances, and dilemmas that life throws at them. Reading through the chapters is like narrative therapy, with the storyteller being the expert who chooses what should be included in the story. Therefore, healing starts and pain ceases, with the evil one being conquered with the Lord's mighty armour."

Joan Bosire, Social Worker
Edmonton, Alberta, Canada.

"Dr. Arku's *Unique You* is a thoughtful exploration of the importance of understanding your purpose in life. She shares personal stories and lessons to help each Christian avoid pitfalls and achieve success in his or her journey through the stages of life. *Unique You* reminds us to always focus on God and the special calling He has placed on each of us as individuals. *Unique You* is a sheer delight to read!"

Alecia L. – Edmonton, Alberta, Canada.

Dedication

This book is dedicated to the many who will discover and live within their purpose, so their lives give glory to God and draw men and women to Christ.

Acknowledgements

To God be all the glory who put these words in my spirit and heart, and for the grace to express them in this book. I'm deeply grateful.

My sincere thanks go to the family of *Inspiring Purpose Academy*, Canada. Your love and appreciation of this ministry, and the many testimonies that we see here, have inspired me to keep sharing God's love and guidance through this book. God bless you.

I'm grateful to my friend and mentor, late Dr. Carmen Vincella Thompson, for always giving me precious nuggets of advice. The guidance and resources you shared with me enriched this book. I know it delights you that I keep on with your legacy of inspiring and building possible futures.

A special thanks to my husband, Professor Frank S. Arku, for supporting and cheering me on to do what is best for my purpose and others, even if it meant that you sacrifice. I am grateful to my children for always being my first audience, listening to my life stories with keen interest and encouraging me.

I thank the University of Alberta (Edmonton, Alberta, Canada) Transition Year Program students who participated in my research and whose stories are reflected in this book.

Finally, I appreciate Shidaanikei Publishers for their exceptional expertise, patience and support throughout this process. Thank you.

Table of Contents

Tables and Figures

Tables:

Figures:

this page Intentionally left blank

Foreword

This thought-provoking book will inspire you to consider and reconsider this sacred life journey we all must embark on. Your life is inscribing a story on earth while you're living and in the annals of heaven. There's hope for every person to write a great story because this is the desire of God. He has made abundant provisions for everyone to be successful, and this book, *Unique You*, is one of the tools God is placing in our hands to compose a great story.

It goes without saying that non-fiction books reflect not only the essence and character of their authors but also tried and tested principles. Having known Dr. Cynthia Arku for a couple of decades, we can testify that this book is from Cynthia's heart to yours. She's the person you gravitate to with your tough and gut-wrenching issues when it feels like your soul is drifting in a bone-dry desert. She's not the calibre that would just prescribe rituals and the recital of perfunctory prayers to persons in distress. Cynthia's deep commitment to God is to see divine mandates fulfilled in people. This is so palpably authentic, and even more sublime when a need arises.

She'll travail for you and with you, if it is a celebration, she's your cheerleader.

This book is Cynthia's clarion call to all generations that every person has a purpose to discover and fulfill. It is not so much about the grandiosity that your purpose in life expresses as it is the fulfillment of a divine mandate.

This book will help you to dial in, edit and fine-tune your purpose in life. Its message clearly reveals that every single human is of utmost value to God, and it is never too late to catch a purpose and fulfill it, because there is a divine inspiration that is beckoning to every soul, always. The distance between you and your breakthrough may be within the simple inspirational elements of this book.

Dr. Rodney and Mrs. Edwoba Atta-Konadu – Guelph, Ontario.

Preface

"***Whatever the mind can conceive and believe, it can achieve"*** (Napoleon Hill). You're reading about my life's stories on how I discovered my purpose after many years of questioning, confusion, and partial clarity. You will find stories of people I have encountered on this journey, from my doctoral research looking at experiences that spurred transition to university and what I learned.

Of all the things you could learn in school, you're not taught that there are simple step-by-step strategies to help you to discover and live your purpose. Cambridge Dictionary defines purpose as, "Why you do something or why something exists." In essence, your purpose is your practical use in this world, which must align with how God hard-wired you. It appears so natural that you must know and follow your purpose. But this is not always the case and resources that attempt to guide this process are unclear and impractical.

Living a purposeful life in the way God hard-wired you is extremely inspiring, fulfilling, and rewarding. Over the years, I've met people who appeared successful in the eyes of the world. But some quit their career, even though they were doing well and earning a great living. Why? Because that career didn't align with how God hard-wired them.

I also think of Jeremy in his 20s who was raised by a foster mother when he was eight. He was nurtured in so much care, love, and discipline in this foster family of a social worker. After many years, he chose to leave home at the age of 15. Jeremy said that he had developed an interest in becoming a social worker as well. Upon second thought, he wanted to figure out his life on his own and make his own decisions to be whatever he desired, not a social worker. About two years of living homeless, he had picked up self-harming habits from friends and acquaintances in the malls and streets (personal communication, February 2014).

Some of Jeremy's friends who knew of his exceptional upbringing couldn't believe that he chose another life – a life of drugs, alcohol, and sleeping on the streets. What might have happened? Jeremy said, "I wanted to find myself. That life is not mine" (personal communication, February 2014). He felt lost. He desired to discover his own purpose to live it. First thing first: Does Jeremy have the tools to discover his purpose?

This book discusses circumstances that hold us from living within our unique purpose. It positions you within God's grand purpose that gives you dominion over all things He created. You become more aware of where you're from, who you're, where you're going, and why you're on earth. Knowing why you're on earth not only exposes you to God's grand purpose for all of humanity but also shows you your specific, practical use or what you must do as an individual - that is your specific purpose - to contribute to accomplishing God's grand purpose.

Next, I guide you through a self-inquiry to take stock of your unique abilities, potentials, passions, and pains, and to create a photographic Purpose Statement that summarizes your purpose along with matching activities and goals. Together, these become your roadmap to achieving this discovered purpose. Nonetheless, I alert you about unexpected tasks, not in your set goals, that may demand you to act and need your careful consideration and flexibility.

Further, I guide you on how to align your discovered purpose with important life decisions, including career, education, and relationships (e.g., courtship, marriage, and friendships). This is because these decisions and relationships make or break your purpose. Therefore, you must carefully assess, consider, pray, and then act on them to live your purpose.

For me, once I discovered that inspiring and guiding others to live their own purpose has always brought huge joy to my life, I knew that it was time to get on track to write this book. Have you experienced the joy of living out the great endowments that God has put in you?

Discovering and living your purpose brings tremendous value to others. You feel deeply in love with yourself as you enjoy what you do so well. You're self-motivated every day and in harmony within because what you do matches God's purpose for your life. Your value brings you provision. You become a channel of help to the world around you and afar. You challenge yourself. You're focused. Your challenges don't break you. Therefore, your life tells a story of triumph since your trust remains in God in all things. The world is attracted to your testimony and success, and they want to know about your Christ. This is the proof that transforms the world.

Today, if this book challenges you to discover and live your purpose, you're doing exactly what it is designed to do. Thanks to the late Dr. Myles Munroe, Dr. Yonggi Cho, and Joyce Meyer whose works have also informed this book. Dr. Munroe said, "Your joy, influence, prosperity is in your purpose." I trust that as you discover and live out your purpose through this simple step-by-step guide in this book, you will no longer live in mediocrity, not using all that is in you.

I trust that by using the tools here, you're inspired, and you will guide others to a purpose-centred life to bring you and others greater value.

this page Intentionally left blank

Introduction

How will this book help you to discover and live your purpose?

- Have you been a Christian for a long while and feeling confused because nothing you have learned has worked or gone your way?
- Are you feeling lost and not sure of your gifts and talents when attempting to choose a career, school, training or entering a relationship?
- Have you felt out of place several months or years into a college or university program that you initially liked?
- Are you busy doing a few jobs to pay the bills, but hear a little voice inside you telling you to do something else more exciting and fulfilling?
- Do you want people to cheer you on in the decisions you've made, but hardly find those cheerleaders, and this is affecting you?

- Do you want to help people within your circle of influence or organization to live their purpose, but you haven't found the right resources to guide them?

This practical, insightful, and easy to read book is for you and your loved ones, if you answered yes to any of these questions.

This book:

- ✓ Will help you to start living your life's purpose sooner than later.
- ✓ Will direct you to reflect and reorganize your path for greater success, without letting others steer you away from your own purpose.
- ✓ Will guide you to plan your life and align every effort to achieve the life that God hard-wired you to have.
- ✓ Will help you to experience a more rewarding Christian life by being intentional in living your true self – your purpose.

- ✓ Will assist you to avoid repeating costly common mistakes in your purposeful journey on earth.
- ✓ Will help you to uncover the knowledge that leaders of organizations need to support employees to achieve their full potential and organizational goals.

In this book, you have easy to follow, clear and concise guidance, which you can master with ease, live, and teach to others how to become purpose-centred. This book takes you into greater joy, fulfillment, and will impact yours and other people's lives as you live your unique purpose.

Who Should Read this Book?

This book is for everyone: *youth, young adults, adults, parents, guardians, teachers, mentors, coaches, human resource practitioners, leaders, and educators* - who desire to unleash their own life's purpose and those of others; something that schools, training institutions and churches don't adequately offer. Business and human resources leaders will find this resource extremely useful for supporting employees to achieve their goals and full potential.

this page Intentionally left blank

Chapter 1

The Winding Road to Discovering Your Purpose

You go out to the woods to observe and learn about rocks with your Grade 3 class. In this adventure, you dig the ground expecting to land on something spectacular; sounds like kid's archeology or geology. You discovered a special pebble. You were sure that this is a stone of special value. You brought it home to show off your find. Not even your siblings could escape your unending telling of your appreciation of this pebble until each one has expressed a gigantic sense of awe for your new discovery. ***Their opinion means the world to you, but your joy from making a great discovery is what matters the most to you.***

That night the pebble became your new bedmate. It laid under your pillow, and you kept admiring it until you didn't know when you fell asleep. Even in your sleep, you catch yourself checking on this new pebble, the love of your life.

It is interesting that when it comes to our purpose in life, many people go through a season of uncertainty or sheer confusion. We don't take time to discover or get excited (like the Grade 3 child) about ourselves. It feels like what you already know becomes a point of doubt. What you know from your intuition becomes a source of anguish. You will be content if someone can affirm or disapprove of your thoughts so that at least you feel that you have had a second opinion to settle things in your mind. Sometimes, a second opinion can be unsettling.

Regardless, you can discover and achieve your purpose if you choose to take the appropriate steps forward. There is hope for us to be able to discover our purpose no matter our life situation today. **"You will either step forward into growth or you will step back into safety"** (Abraham Maslow).

In this chapter, I will expose the difficulties in our world and the body of Christ that have made this book necessary. I look at various seasons we experience on the journey seeking to discover ourselves. Further, we explore reasons many people live outside their life's purpose, pointing to the influence of friends, church, associations, and community in which we spend time. This is so that we fill the knowledge gap and don't suffer wasting any more time before we discover and live our purpose.

'Feeling Lost'?

Who? Lost? How? Can't figure it out, right? This is the youth or adult who is struggling to accept some of the ***I can't-believe-this-happened-to-me*** moments. You're full of unanswered questions. Who can help me unravel my own life to know why I exist or my use? I thought this was a given for everyone; you come into this life and do something with your life to survive and thrive. Well, it is not so. You must know certain important things to guide you onto the right path.

For me, I followed flimsy ideas or what others told me I can do. Sometimes, I worked with the opportunities that came my way. It was not until I started attending university that I realized I needed to give this thought a serious commitment of time.

Like most children, I also had those ideas of what I wanted to be when I grew up. It was fancy as a child growing up in Ghana to say: doctor, lawyer, engineer, and the likes. Perhaps it is still the same today. As for me, I was fascinated by the idea of travelling in the skies. Then, I heard a fancy word: air hostess (i.e., flight attendant). The name, air hostess, sounded so nice. Imagine, I was learning new vocabulary and came across one that sounded phonetically snooty and spectacular. I figured it must be that one. I heard others say they wanted to be a pilot and thought, that's them.

Being an air hostess was about the most glamourous, coolest, and prestigious career on my mind. I recall having encountered disposable plates, little bowls and cutlery used in the plane at various points and felt a great connection that way. In a big way, going on the plane to the white man's land, which flowed with milk and honey, was riveting for this 10-year-old me. Everyone wants a great life, so I figured for me this is how to attain it.

I don't recall ever seeing an air hostess or flight attendant at the time. My passion would have gone through the roof had I seen one sooner. I would have been even more fascinated by their gorgeous dressing in the cutest uniforms, modelling those missy high heels and pulling along immaculate travel bags descending from the plane with the crew.

Even without this catchy scenery, I persisted to become this air hostess until several years later in middle school, I let go of this flimsy idea not grounded on serious thought and adequate information. This is part of what it means to be growing up. You get lost from time to time.

Feeling lost is a reality that gets worse, especially for those who have little to no points of reference within their circles of family, friends, and church or even school connections about such important matters. The circle of influence usually shapes the direction we take in the decisions we make. As a result, you remain neutral about important decisions or worst yet, take an uninformed position on important matters. This puts you in a state of confusion or error. You may be well connected with people of influence who are your role models, and still feel lost. Also, pressure from parents or guardians or people to whom your loyalty is important, wanting you to follow a certain path, can be another source of unease.

One thing that baffles me is how a person can pretend to be enjoying something for so long. I was in disbelief hearing the story of a promising young man choosing a career. Yatzy said he had lied to his parents that he wanted to be a medical doctor all through his early schooling. This is because that's what they wanted for him. It was when he was about to apply for his university education that he revealed his true career passion for economics.

I wondered how he felt anticipating a completely different career when he was in elementary, middle, and high school while talking around the kitchen table towards a false dream: to become a medical doctor. There was a big disconnect between what he wanted to pursue and what his parents wished for him.

Types of 'Feeling Lost'

"The greatest tragedy is life without purpose" (Dr. Myles Munroe). I will use the analogy or likeness of shoes to illustrate the types of 'feeling lost' situations. There are various types of "feeling lost:'

1. Wearing someone else's shoes (Type 1)
2. Not finding a fitting pair of shoes (Type 2)
3. Found a pair of shoes that fits, but is not your style (Type 3).

Type 1 involves wearing shoes that are not yours, yet because you love the shoes, for the time being, you decide you will enjoy wearing them. In fact, you won't even know it is someone else's shoes because they appear to fit so well. Here, your circumstances have made you believe in a purpose that is not inherently or naturally you. But by adoption, you've accepted this purpose. A close examination of your thoughts and feelings tells you that you're off track.

Type 2 includes those who may be looking to get shoes but want to make sure they fit well. You're not sure if there is a pair of shoes you would like, because so far none of the shoes you've found fit. The problem is this: you're looking for what you love but in the wrong places. You're looking outwardly rather than inwardly.

Type 3 is where you've found shoes that fit you well and you're comfortable in them. However, you're unsure if you like the style. In this group, you've done all you know to discover your purpose. You like the choices you're making. You've made some choices of activities that align with your purpose. But every now and then you think there is something more that you look forward to experiencing. Unfortunately, several people are in this group.

One theme that runs across type 1, type 2 and type 3 groups is that all of them are unsettled.

- **Do you find yourself or others in any of these three groups?**

We face many pressures along with inadequate information to make important decisions that might not put us on the path of our purpose. In the next section, let's go deeper to look at how and reasons people feel unsettled outside their purpose.

Friends Got Me Lost

How about if those friends said, you got them lost? Following the crowd can sometimes be a good thing if the crowd leads you closer to your purpose. The issue is not about good or bad company. Obviously, hanging around a bad company of friends will get you to experience, do and try things that corrupt your character and purpose.

With every association comes influence. Many have followed others blindly because they agreed with whatever activities they were involved in. It appeared okay in that moment or season of life. They say: **Show me who your friends are, and I will know who you're becoming?**

Wrong associations can cause deep spiritual problems. You wonder why you're hardly able to break away from your indecent friends. It is, as though, Satan, the enemy, builds on your natural weaknesses – on your weak vulnerable mind. Out of the natural weakness, not setting principles for ourselves or non-adherence to principles we set for ourselves, we give in to the flesh. ***The enemy is aware that you chose the wrong associations because you ignored and continue to ignore the intuition of the Holy Spirit.***

You were too immature or lacked the knowledge to know *your destiny* (i.e., destiny is a state, end or future that seemingly has been decided beforehand - Merriam Webster) or *your purpose* (which is your practical use God intended for you). Annette Walker, author of the *Destiny Point Experience* says destiny is "something specific God has for you to accomplish in this life" – similar to your specific purpose.

You may be too ignorant about the difference between destiny destroyers or destiny builders. As a believer, living your purpose is a threat to the enemy. The job of impeding your purpose, and impact is closer to being accomplished if the enemy can get you to choose the wrong friends.

> *"For if you live according to the flesh, you will die; but if by the Spirit you put to death the deeds of the body, you will live"* (Romans 8: 13).

The flesh conflicts with the spirit. Colossians 3: 5, urges that we "Put to death, therefore, whatever belongs to your earthly nature" such as sexual immorality, impurity, lust, evil desires and greed" and the list goes on and on. But we also know that the enemy is on duty 24/7 setting up ways for the believer to falter, and for the unbeliever to remain without believing in Christ.

The enemy makes sure that you're stuck with wrong friendships to get the job done. When you get so enmeshed with them, you can hardly differentiate between right from wrong (holy from unholy); both become blurred in your thinking. This is where you have developed a heart that is so seared, toughened and hardened, so much so that you can't sense the Holy Spirit nudging you to "look closely, see the danger and flee."

1 Peter 5: 8 instructs us:

> *"Stay alert! Watch out for your great enemy, the devil. He prowls around like a roaring lion, looking for someone to devour."*

The enemy's assignment is to make sure you never break away. Your flesh taking pleasure in sin makes his work easier. His goal is for your great purpose and future to be devoured.

Amid being trapped because of reckless living, you may think about your great dreams, but narrowly see the barriers to achieving them. You're preoccupied with thinking about how stuck life is for you. You get frustrated that your dreams have remained unfulfilled. The frustration gets you into an unhealthy mental state. You feel so worthless, but that is a lie you've believed because your self-worth doesn't depend on your circumstance(s). Then, you don't care about anything. You no longer mind if your life goes nowhere.

In those difficult times, you may have moments of awakening where you desire to turn things around and get back to making your dreams or purpose

count, but how? You wonder where to begin. How do I catch up is what some may ask as if life is a race? Thinking in this manner gets you into more trouble if you're trying to catch up (in a race), but with whom?

Who will come to your rescue? God, Himself helps us in His word and power, as well as uses people to help us.

> *"No weapon formed against you shall prosper, And every tongue which rises against you in judgment You shall condemn. This is the heritage of the servants of the LORD, And their righteousness is from Me," Says the LORD"* (Isaiah 54: 17).

Therefore, the power in Christ delivers you when you take Christ's forgiveness, believe, and speak the word of God in faith. This frees you from being dominated by natural desires and the enemy's influence. The Bible provides guidance centred on the workings of the Holy Spirit. With the Holy Spirit, the word of God comes alive and steers your life unto freedom and holiness.

Our friends can help us in those tough times, too; however, do they have the skills to successfully steer us to our purpose? ***Devoted Christian friends with good intentions still might not take you where you want to be***. Why? Because I have seen people associating deeply with their church groups and in healthy activities who still haven't found themselves any closer to living their purpose after several decades. The tendency is to hang around people just like you, and not those who are knowledgeable in the area where you need help. Such well-meaning people may or may not point you in the right direction of discovering yourself and your purpose.

Several promising brothers and sisters in Christ live in regret for not understanding how to apply the scriptures and the Holy Spirit to an intentionally purpose-led life. They may neglect the place of the spirit of wisdom, which is so essential**.**

Alice was a zealous sister in the Lord with a fabulous life in front of her. She spent most of her time in senior high school with zealous friends like herself, camping in prayer forests, seeking the face of God, and wasn't sure if this helped her purpose. She made costly mistakes by not continuing her education because she didn't listen to wise counsel. Seeking God and His presence is good practice for the Christian who wants the fullness of God's love and power. But there is a place for wise counsel, too.

> *But for those who don't have guidance (from wisdom) on how to tap into the Spirit of God to navigate their purpose and to accomplish it, they face big challenges. This creates a false sense that God is incapable of producing a blessed life in all things. It is not so at all!*

Looking at her life again, Alice later figured that 'this Jesus thing probably works for only certain people.' She thought if I couldn't find anything to do after high school, I must as well get married. At the time, it felt like this was the greatest accomplishment within her circle of friends in church. Five years into her marriage, Alice realized that something was missing in her life. Her husband's promise to care for her and her three children wasn't enough; she had no valuable skills to support her family's livelihood.

Besides, the abuse of each other got worse, and the marriage was on the verge of collapse. Alice's eyes were wide open when she saw her colleagues back in the day doing those things (in careers) that she wished she could do or perceived could do better, given that she did well academically than some of them. She questioned where her life was going – 'what did I do wrong? Would I ever get somewhere decent in life?'

I wonder what those friends or schoolmates might be thinking of Alice. Perhaps, they too are saying to themselves: "Alice and others were the cause of their misguided and unsettled lives." Alice's friends didn't have the wisdom that she needed as a teenager, nor did she possess the counsel that her friends needed for coming into alignment with their purpose – if they knew it.

So, you see, you may have a role and others, too, may have contributed to the difficult life you've faced living outside your purpose. And the main reasons may include ignorance; wrong associations; fleshy desires; the enemy's work; and inexperienced friends and connections.

- ***You're not hopeless. If you've been made, you can be remade***

It will take a new way to pull yourself out of the mess or to get yourself on your unique track. A better life is possible regardless of these challenges and other distractions that might have occurred.

Chapter 2

Distractions of Early Sexual Experimentation

Can I have a girlfriend or boyfriend as a young person and still be on course with my purpose? What about adults? Today, keeping a sexually intimate relationship appears common amongst some young people. As a young person still maturing with various challenges and responsibilities, this is one less trouble to refrain from. Life is already full of distractions, you step into new phases and new things as you grow. Not guarding your heart and mind carefully makes you a victim. However, you can navigate this from a position of victory by your holy living. In this chapter, I will look at the various dangers we face and how our expectations are sometimes not met to put us on the path of our life's purpose.

Did Someone See My Struggle?

We are surrounded by some who are ready to help us even if others are uninterested. Some are quick to compare you with others, find faults and reprimand you. Others watch our lives, not as mentors or coaches, but to take pleasure at our missteps and use us as an avoidable example.

The heart of the natural man or woman can be insecure and unsupportive. It takes a heart filled with the Holy Spirit to always desire the well-being of another. Perhaps it is easier to want your relative to do well in life because it is in the interest of the family. In certain situations, some can be disinterested in the well-being of even their family members.

Also, spectating people's lives to find fault due to their insecurity can bring extreme pressure on others. We are blessed with amazing helpers as well. You find cheerleaders who applaud you and share those great moments of success with you. But those spectating with low expectations for you become a heavy weight. But sometimes their negative attitudes motivate you to want to prove them wrong, which also brings more pressure on you.

Additionally, the pressures in elementary, junior and senior high school and the temptation of sexual experimentation distract dreams or purposes. Sexual relationships come with very powerful emotions and could interfere with your studies requiring mastery of balancing your emotions and mind. No wonder some young people begin pleasing their sexual urge, then, end up dropping their studies. Some have dropped out of high or even junior high school because of the traps of sex and sexual experimentation.

I call this 'sexual experimentation' because this is not meant for young unmarried people. The Bible is clear that sexual activities are only permitted in marriage. Allowing your hormonal changes and attractions to take you into sexual involvements (such as masturbation, pornography, and internet or phone sex), and indecent lifestyles hinder your purpose.

Further, as a keen observer of youths, I have seen that young people are more likely to resist authority during this time. They resist the authority of their parents or guardians at home, and of teachers and leaders at school or church, because of their involvement in some of these secret or open sins. It wasn't surprising when I saw videos on WhatsApp (social media) of high school students making profane utterances alluding to sexual experiences that they have had. It was troubling to see such indecent acts on social media. But they were involved in those acts because the power of sin was fueling it.

There is a reason God kept sexual relations in marriage because I imagine He anticipated that the couple will be capable of managing this in a healthy way. This will coexist harmoniously among other obligations such as working, caring for children, and training.

A gun in the hands of an immature, stubborn, ungodly young person more likely leads to the death of his or her dreams. That's what these involvements do. They distract and confuse priorities. Often, the young person is more likely to give in to the sexual draws because that is the enemy's best option to complete the job of killing his or her dreams.

I think of school friends and mates who stifled their dreams and continued on the path of confusion because of early sexual involvements. The determined ones retook their qualifying exams (to make it into college or university), due to prior avoidable distractions and delays.

Moreover, for adults who fall for sexual temptations, their dreams can become twisted. "A kingdom that is divided against itself cannot stand" (Mark 3:24). To be divided is to set your mind on something else other than your purpose in life. And if the enemy can have you preoccupied with useless, mundane things of no substantial value to distract your purpose, that's what he goes for.

As a result, you would find yourself doing everything that won't lead you anywhere meaningful. ***Your energy, mind, heart, soul, abilities, and skills are divided, so you can't build anything fulfilling and rewarding that complements your practical use in this world. Allowing your fleshly desires to win is a catalyst for messing up dreams and purpose.***

You don't obtain the clarity that is guaranteed from the Holy Spirit when you cherish and toy with sin; the Holy Spirit stays away from you.

> *"And do not grieve the Holy Spirit of God, by whom you were sealed for the day of redemption"* (Ephesians 4:30)

The Holy Spirit departs from you when you grieve or sadden Him with sinning. You don't have God's help.

Then, your efforts may appear to be yielding some results, but you aren't getting anything close to what God has for you if you diligently seek and walk in His ways. Sin distracts you and you can hardly see your way ahead into your future or live in your purpose if you know it. Christ has made a way for us; when we repent from our sins. A brand-new, clean page starts because all our sins are forgiven. Suppose we expected people's help on our way to guide us to our purpose, sometimes, we may be waiting for a long while. In the next section, let's look at how people attempt to help in this and how far that help goes.

I Screamed, Lost! No One Came

It is easy to blame adults for getting lost or feeling lost and outside your purpose. We live on the assumption that age correlates with wisdom or understanding of the essence of our being. This is not always so.

Job 32:7 says:

> *"I thought, 'Age should speak; advanced years should teach wisdom."*

This servant of God, Job, realized that advancing in age does not always mean a higher level of understanding that can help others. Often, I find that the adult being criticized didn't know the way to live his or her purpose, too. It is like blaming the blind person for getting you where you didn't want to go. It is reasonable to expect those that have had a lot of life experience and are passionate about this subject matter to guide you onto the right track. Typically, a person has expertise in one or a few areas, without mastery over a broad range of disciplines.

Besides, some of the guidance available are loose theories and less practical ideas for discovering your purpose. ***To believe that an adult can accurately prescribe or dictate your purpose, without your own efforts in systematically discovering it, is best described as a recipe for disaster***. Guidance in discovering your purpose is still an underdeveloped discipline or field, given that people still find it uneasy to discover their own or lead others to discover their purpose.

It is easy for people to form inaccurate theories on this subject from their life experiences. Though they have had a difficult life themselves, they lack the knowledge to draw out lessons to mentor others. This situation creates an understanding that discovering your life's purpose is hard to decipher.

- **You will figure it out as you go, so don't stress it!**

Some of your favourite life coaches, mentors, siblings, and friends might be guiding you through life with good intentions, and still, you feel lost with all that help. What I realize is that guiding someone through this [purpose] discovery is beyond sharing life experiences. You can learn from books, workshops, forums, social media, or family members' life experiences. These kinds of information are helpful for avoiding pitfalls and building your life on the skills, opportunities and advice offered in these sources. However, you will be unclear about your life's purpose especially when the knowledge is NOT PRACTICAL.

Role models, mentors and coaches play a significant role through this aspect of discovery if you share common values with them. These are individuals who have perfected their skills to a larger extent. However, like any human endeavour, there are chances that they can let you down. Perhaps they live or model an aspect of life that disagrees with your own worldview or values. There is an extent to which you follow the path of a role model or mentor. When their values clash with your faith-based values, it usually means that a sphere of confusion is open.

Another kind of discomfort can set in when you have had some learning from others, books, or online resources, and you're ready to put into practice what you learned. *A fascinating reality is that some fear to act after they've gathered so much knowledge.* The moment you want to decide on which career, which program to study, which friends to associate with, then, sometimes you realize you feel inadequate without the confidence to act.

'Big brothers' or 'big sisters' as mentors or coaches who are contributing to shaping the futures of young people and many others are very much in demand today. I remember the story of my new friend, Sam. Sam has so much potential. He misdirected his passions and skills towards mundane, quick-money, ungodly activities, and lifestyle. He emphatically said:

"*You know, the reason why I'm messed up is because there was no mentor.*"

I wondered what Sam meant. He talked about going to church day and night while growing up, often thrice a week. His parents raised him to endear God. He emphasized that his birth was such a delight to his parents. Their greatest joy was for him to grow up in the fear of God and serve God all his life. He pointed out the significance of his name; "this was why my parents named me Sam" (like Samuel's mother dedicated him to the priesthood under the high priest Eli in the Bible).

He added that, during his teenage years, attraction to mundane things set in. He chose to rove with ungodly friends. Sam consulted shrines for satanic powers to back his worldly lifestyle. He wasted many years on fornication, alcoholism, and drugs. He financed this lifestyle from his quick-money schemes.

Today, Sam attributes his previously misguided life to the absence of good mentors.

- Did any adult see Sam's utter mess?

- Couldn't anyone guide him to the right track?
- What did his family or the church folks do about it?

- **Will everyone put all-hands-on-deck to make sure you don't remain lost or even get lost?**

Certainly, we need more mentors and coaches now than ever!

Seldom do some go out of their way to guide, mentor, and coach others struggling outside their purpose. Life can get busy where people are constantly rushing to get to the next pressing thing. Besides, the need can appear extremely complex, so you don't want to rope yourself into an endless problem of others. For some, it is all about survival of the fittest. It is a cat race, so, 'If you don't get ahead, then that's your problem.'

This sense of competition has not served humanity well. ***"It takes a village to raise a child"*** was the African proverb that I heard growing up. So that at least one person from the whole village will come to the rescue of this lost and troubled fellow. Soon, I observed that some people are quick to point out a wrong you're doing instead of offering a helping hand. Thank God for those who watch out for you and others!

School teachers are a tremendous influence on learners who are struggling with discovering their purpose. I was fortunate to have several good teachers. Some were very inspiring as I heard them talking about life. My Ghanaian junior and high school teachers spoke about the future we were likely to have if we do our part well. At the time, I was yet to see the future they were talking about. They spoke about their own preparation for the future that they desired.

Some of these motivational messages were with small groups during a break or class moment, and church service at school. I looked forward to them all through junior high to high school. For students who lacked those wisdom nuggets from family or church, hearing teachers' life stories and seeing them model their journey into a great future was very inspiring.

Looking back, I understood that some teachers also struggled with finding and living their purpose. Years ago, when school punishment was common in many

Ghanaian public schools, some teachers were unnecessarily quick to use the stick to discipline students. Discipline is necessary for every child. Sometimes, this provided temporary relief to a teacher who was frustrated about feeling trapped in a teaching career. Students ended up hating school or dropping out. Thus, students suffer the consequences when teachers are discontented with their lives.

To help you get on your track (if you appear lost outside your purpose) to be contented, usually, people may nudge you quietly. Are you aware of the discord inside the heart and mind of that person you're going to guide back onto the right track?

Going back to Sam's story, suppose you're going to help him:

a. Do you know his life's purpose?
b. Do you know his talents (abilities) or passion?
c. Is he ready or interested in following his purpose to become a better version of himself, if you guide him to discover his purpose?

One of the favourite sayings of my middle school teacher, Dr. Joseph Adonu, which shaped my early life is this: "Where purpose is not known, abuse is inevitable." ***A life without purpose, without a planned destination, goes anywhere or nowhere.*** People not guided by a known purpose respond to every call. Everything is appealing. Must it?

We make various choices that make or break our dreams.

- ***Some miss an opportunity because they don't understand whether it has relevance to their lives.***
- ***Others get so confused they just follow the crowd because it is the easiest way out of confusion, therefore, they take anything that appears to be an opportunity.***
- ***Some agree with every opinion because they don't have established beliefs, principles, values, and desires for themselves and for relating with the world.***
- ***Others agree with anyone or do anything because they want to be friends with everyone.***

Not choosing friends well can endanger the manifestation of your purpose. Many have been invited to friendships or societies that have caused them grief and pain because they showed interest by their agreeable expressions. Or perhaps because they were neither here nor there, neither hot nor cold; they were conflicted. 'Being in the middle makes you vulnerable to the worst situations and consequences. You become an easy target because you don't have a mind of your own; you don't have established values that you're living by.

Thankfully, some discover themselves at some point in their life's journey through tough life lessons. You learn from well-informed and experienced mentors, coaches, family members, friends, and significant others. Such people wish they knew sooner what they came to know later in life. They wished that no one experiences the earlier mess that they experienced, faced, or put themselves through. They wished their children, grandchildren and future generations to obtain clear and better guidance through their self and purpose discovery process.

> *I am one of those people who wish for all these things for many. I am one of those who is grateful that I am*

> *living my purpose. I know that there are still many out there, still left behind and will find this book a clear path forward to living their purpose.*

The road to living your purpose fully can be meandering where we tend to blame others or ourselves for mistakes and delays. However, being able to imagine the beautiful possible future that you could have could turn you around. Imagination is key to living your purpose. Like praying, you can have what you imagine (Ephesians 3:20). Have we abandoned our power of imagination? In the next chapter, I explore the potential of your imagination and how this is a vital part of your purpose-centred life.

Chapter 3

What Happened to Your Imagination?

H***ave you walked into your future to see how spectacular it is?*** Have you walked into your future to see your great husband or beautiful wife of your dreams? You live in this nice house or apartment with your two or three lovely children all doing well in school. Your spouse has a good-paying stress-free job and so do you. Once a year, you go on a mission trip for winning souls, mentoring new believers or pastors, and building schools. You go on vacation annually with your family. Your family including your children are loving and serving God. Can you see this future? Can you see the life you desire? If you can see it, you can have it! Unfortunately, we are neglecting the power of our imagination to our disadvantage.

In this chapter, let's look at the potential hidden in your imagination, and what tapping into this treasure will do for you. I will show you how God speaks to you through your imagination. Also, I will explain why you must be skilled at imagining while taking actions to bring those great imaginations that support your life's purpose.

Imagination is Your Eye into Your Future

Merriam-Webster Dictionary defines imagination as "the act or power of forming a mental image of something, not present to the senses … It is a creative ability." Seeing or imagining is having an image of the end state you desire. *Your imagination is your eye into your tomorrow and future.* Many of us have tried various things in our attempt to discover ourselves.

- ***Could knowing or seeing someone in a career that you desire assure you (to an extent) that your dreams are possible?***

- ***Is it normal to see what the finished meal looks like on the menu before the chef starts cooking it when at the restaurant?***

Knowing or seeing someone who inspires you to follow in his or her footsteps is certainly a tremendous source of inspiration.

However, one fundamental ingredient to a purposeful life is your imagination. You must have a ***powerful imagination.*** A lack of a powerful imagination is the reason for the many failures you're not so proud of. Imagination is a strong force for achieving our dreams, but for some of us, imagination must be bolstered by tangible evidence of people (you know and see) who are already what we desire. Others are great dreamers. They start moving on to their dreams quickly.

You need more than seeing eyes for your '*purpose to live.*' You may not always see or connect with those mentors, coaches and role models already doing what you aspire or desire to become. That's why living your life with a 'seeing (with the physical eyes) is believing mentality' is not an ideal approach for a Christian. If your walk with God is a faith walk, then, you must tap into your imaginative capacities to see your aspirations. Using your imagination along with the Holy Spirit pulls in all other resources you need for your life's purpose to manifest.

The absence of powerful imagination means you can't see your future. What you imagine is what you have. This is the faith dimension! If our imagination is neglected in this quest to live within our purpose, we are in trouble! Next, let's look at why your imagination is a force that you must engage with for your purpose to be established.

Your Imagination is Your Gold, So Mine It!

The Holy Spirit uses your imagination or what you see in your mind to create your reality in Christ. ***A dead imagination is a mind not tapping into its powerful ability to envision and realize the reason you exist, your use or your purpose.***

God knows that we must see what we ask for, so He provided examples for us in the Bible. God used what I call objects of faith. The objects of faith are real items or experiences that prove the existence of what we are asking for in the mind, heart, and spirit before we can pray them into reality.

Visions and dreams are objects of our faith. A vision is when you see people and things in a trance or with your eyes open as a supernatural experience; it is a dream when you see such while asleep. When you have the Holy Spirit active in you, your dreams and visions are filled with important messages for you. Our visions and dreams are sight gifts that reveal secrets and provide vital information for now and the future. When you use them well, you have clear directions and tangible outcomes.

> *I think of the popular concept of meditation in yoga and other eastern religions where people imagine their reality through various levels of meditation. This concept is not new to God.*

Does God Use Imaginations for Your Own Good?

God used visions and dreams to help the people of the Old Testament in the Bible to see their future and the promises He has made to them. God showed Abraham in visions the blessings that He has provided. Abraham and his nephew, Lot, were prosperous in Bethel among the Canaanites and Perizzites land where they lived. Their possessions were so great that they were unable to stay together in the same place. Lot's herdsmen were mixing up with each other and risking quarrels, therefore, they decided to part ways.

Abraham asked Lot to pick the side of the land that he wanted. After Lot chose the best land and parted from him, God spoke to Abraham about the Promised Land that he and his descendants will have:

> "[14]*The Lord said to Abram after Lot had parted from him, "**Look** around from where you are, to the north and south, to the east and west.* [15]*All the land that you* **see** *I will give to you and your offspring forever"* (Genesis 13: 14-15).

God wanted Abraham to see the beautiful, prosperous, and well-nourished land in his imagination. Abraham didn't travel to the physical location God was talking about; the conversation was happening in a spiritual dimension or realm in a vision. God said to Abraham: ***Look**...[**and**]....**see***....Had He just told Abraham about this land without him seeing it, Abraham might find it difficult to believe and hold on to the promise.

So, God gave him a preview or a revelation of the land. The vision experience allowed Abraham to get a feel and sense of the nature of the land that God promised. God had an agenda - He wanted Abraham to have a clear image of the land He had promised him.

In another instance, God showed Abraham in a vision the children he will have:

> [4]*Then the word of the Lord came to him: "This man will not be your heir, but a son who is your own flesh and blood will be your heir."* [5]*He took him outside and said, "**Look** up at the sky and **count** the stars—if indeed you can count them." Then he said to him, "So shall your offspring be"* (Genesis 15: 4 -5).

Again, God emphasized the need to see when he told Abraham to ***'look'...***at the stars in a *vision*. God instructed Abraham to '***count***' them; to do such a meticulous task of counting stars in a sub-conscious, supernatural realm. I am sure after Abraham saw the stars and got tired of counting what was the equivalent of the number of children that he was going to have, he became fully persuaded. He no longer doubted God's promise because he had *a clear picture in his mind of his many children* whenever he looks up and saw the stars. Abraham and his wife, Sarah, had Isaac. From this child of promise, this one seed, Isaac, bore the *12 tribes of Israel*. Indeed, he became the father of many children (descendants) and nations as God promised by the count of the stars.

While God still gives dreams and visions to us, not everyone hears (sees) from God in this way. But we can all imagine or use our imaginative capacities to help our faith to see our great desires, goals, aspirations, and future.

THE LESSON IS THIS:

- **God wants us to be able to look and see our desires in our conscious (physical mind) and subconscious (supernatural mind)**.

It becomes difficult to have a desire or future that you can't see in your imagination. ***"Logic will get you from A to Z; imagination will get you everywhere"*** (Albert Einstein). Let's look at some more practical workings of our imagination for attaining our purpose.

Bring Back Your Imagination to Work

Your purpose relies on your imagination to become a reality, so get it engaged, and get it to work for you. Imagination is the greatest gift that God gave to all humans. The power of imagination works for:

1. *A vain person* or pursuits outside the will of God, and
2. *The believer*'s (in Christ) pursuits within the will of God.

In this section, let's look at how powerful and weak imaginations work. Further, I explain the believer's advantage; how your *hope, faith, the Holy Spirit, and imagination* work together to produce the outcomes that you desire.

Powerful Imaginations versus Weak Imaginations

Your imagination produces mighty results for you as a believer in Christ. Do you wonder how several *nonbelievers* (in Christ) have achieved dreams without relying on God's power?

The following scenarios demonstrate the workings of powerful and weak imaginations -

Scenario 1: Powerful imagination: example of an unbeliever

This woman doesn't believe in Christ: *She dreams of living a luxurious, stress-free life. Her desire is to marry a good man with her family living in a modern luxurious ranch home in the suburb. She dreams to have a high-caliber sports car, Lamborghini, with four other automotive 'toys.' From that moment, she is excited about her future.*

In her sleep, she starts to dream about the husband, future home, car, and other automotive toys. She repeatedly sees the details of her great life within the eyes of her imagination. To take this further, she cut out from magazines images of the car, house, husband, and the expensive toys she desires. She posts the pictures on the walls of the living room, bedroom, and kitchen of her small one-bedroom old apartment. She has similar small-sized pictures inserted in her purse as well.

Every time she sees the pictures, she sees herself walking around the ranch. She also sees her husband driving this dream car on their way to her favourite hockey game. She continues to have a foretaste of her dream life just by constantly rolling those pictures in her mind or imagination. She is focused and her undivided energy is bringing those dreams to fruition. Because she is ***SEEING*** *the dream constantly and subconsciously living it in her imagination, she selected and pursued opportunities matching her dreams.*

She eventually lives this wealthy and contented lifestyle she has dreamt about and imagined. This may not be your dream or imagination; you have your unique one.

Let's see a weak imagination.

Scenario 2: Weak imagination: example of a believer

This man believes in Christ: *He neglected the tools that God has given him to imagine and bring those magnificent imaginations to reality. He didn't imagine anything he desires, not to give herself a chance to dream about them. He prays vaguely asking whatever God desires for him. He can't remember the last time he saw in his thoughts, subconscious or around him an image or picture of the career, wife, family, ministry that he may like. He is* ***NOT SEEING*** *his dream if any. He finds it difficult to describe to his friends, colleagues, family member, or pastor* *what he desires in life. He doesn't pray about any specific thing or person for more than a minute. He doesn't track any testimonies from anything happening in his life that is extraordinary or routine.*

He follows the force and direction of the wind because there are no certain or clear goals. He jumps on to anything that appears an opportunity. Sometimes, he ignores an opportunity he is not expecting – after all he didn't pray for that specific opportunity. He spends his time anyhow, not into any specific imaginations because he didn't have.

What do you think will be the result of such underused imagination capacity he has? Mediocrity of course! His life will be nothing close to what is possible if he used his imagination more fully.

You must hope for things or a specific outcome in your imagination. One of my favourite Scriptures is:

> *"For in this hope we were saved. But hope that is seen is no hope at all. Who hopes for what they already have?"* (Romans 8: 24).

Hope here suggests that there is an expectation of a future good that is you're yet to have. So, the hope is not seen.

This means that I don't have to see this hope (of tomorrow or the future) with my physical eyes. This is because the moment I see it, it is no longer hope. ***Hope is an expectation I have of something in my imagination.***

What does the Bible say about the way your faith in Christ must work?

> *"Now faith is the substance of things hoped for, the evidence of things not seen"* (Hebrews 11:1).

a. ***Faith is the 'substance' of hope.***
b. ***Faith is the 'evidence' that can't be seen.***

To use faith, you hold on to 'substance' and 'evidence;' you must create the substance and evidence in your mind and around you. Those images or pictures in her mind, on the wall, and in her purse are the 'substance' and 'evidence' of those desires or dreams that the *woman in scenario 1* had even though she is not a Christian.

You're acting on faith by using those items to connect you with your dreams.

- If you undermine the power of your imagination, then God is not responsible for your faith that is not working for you.

But you must apply knowledge (insight and understanding) to your faith (2 Peter 1: 5).

> *When you haven't seen but you hope for something (not yet at hand), by connecting to a visual image of that thing or person in your imagination, you've moved those things into the physical realm; all things are yours and you will see them in a matter of time because of your powerful imagination.*

So, you see, your imagination is also your eyesight. Your imagination replaces a natural optical sight.

- The blindness of your physical eyes is not so much an issue as blindness of your imaginative eyes.

- What robs you is the lack of discipline to apply your imagination to see, touch, feel, and smell the (ready-to-be-delivered) those pleasant desires, passions, dreams, and life as finished products (results or outcomes).

- Make your imagination practical, so you can see it or touch it or speak to it even as images, to build faith for that desired outcome.

Moreover, a believer's imagination goes beyond the natural seeing of mental pictures or images. When a Christian is filled with the Holy Spirit, imagination flows out of the Holy Spirit because your renewed nature, now led by the Holy Spirit, steers your desires, passions, dreams, and life.

> *As I became more attuned with the Holy Spirit, I realize the ease with which I enter visions and dreams to see the way Abraham saw God's promises of the prosperous land and his many children.*

❖ ***When your mind has become a magnet of spiritual sights because of constant practice of imagining God's truth, imagining your desires, and those of others,' you're taken to the 'stock room of God' where you're able to have a foretaste or preview of the outcomes you desire supernaturally. Your mind and spirit are always ready to make the right choices to accomplish the outcome you desire.***

We have seen that applying imagination to your hope, faith and knowledge powered by the Holy Spirit gives you greater results. Imagination is only one of many elements you need; you must be aware of your unique endowments and expect a unique purpose so that you don't expect to have the same purpose as another.

Unique You, Embrace Your Uniqueness

You're a unique human being with special gifts, talents, passions, potentials, and experiences that shape your imaginations and purpose. Just as our imaginations are unique and a wonder to others, so are our purposes. When you tap into the power of imagination, you become everything God made you to be.

No two lives are the same, and no two imaginations are the same – that is the truth about your nature. David in the Bible, described as a 'man after God's own heart,' said:

> *"I praise you, for I am fearfully and wonderfully made. Wonderful are your works; my soul knows it very well"* (Psalm 139: 14).

Since you're fearfully and wonderfully made, it is likely that:

- ✓ I'm in awe when I see certain things about you.
- ✓ I'm astounded when I hear your voice.
- ✓ I'm speechless when you touch me.
- ✓ I'm amazed when you do some things that I can't do. And the list goes on.

You're indeed a wonder to me because I know only myself well or perhaps not even so well. And I realize you're so different from me in a few or many ways, even though you and I have biological similarities such as blood in our veins, or that we laugh when something is funny or feel sad when we lose a loved one.

People must wonder about your purpose because you're not like them – you don't have the exact same endowments and are not heading on the same path to fulfillment or prosperity. They are not familiar with your uniqueness. When they look in the mirror carefully, they see themselves, not you, no matter how hard they attempt to draw a comparison between you and themselves. Also, they see that you're different from them.

I Corinthians 4: 7,

> *"For who makes you differ from another? And what do you have that you did not receive? Now if you did indeed receive it, why do you boast as if you had not received it?"*

Apostle Paul acknowledged that we are different because of how we have been made by God, not necessarily out of our own creation.

Therefore, it is alright to feel lost because you're different and unique from that person who appears to have gone the path you desire. Though you may appear similar in desires, you're still different and unique in various ways. Therefore, your paths in this life will differ as well. ***No one is packaged like you and that is why 'only you can figure you out.*** You're on your way, get excited!

That's why it is not a condition that you must see or know someone living your kind of a dream, imagination, and purpose before embarking on yours. Having someone's life as a reference point (or a guinea pig or a model) builds confidence. Following the steps of a particular graphic designer, preacher, engineer, president and nurse, a great father or mother figure is alright. You can chart your own path.

What makes life adventurous and exciting is that you may never know what exactly is at the end of one marathon journey, but we know the result will be good. Follow the exact steps someone used for arriving at their aspirations. You can have similar results but not the same result. Why? Everyone is unique and so are the means and outcomes of your actions.

Often, modelling with computers to predict the future on a particular matter leaves room for difference or deviation. Since social processes can change easily, so do the results. That's why feeling lost symbolizes that you're unique and no one knows you well and that you want to discover and know some things that are unique about you.

Only God knows you well. Only God knows all things.

> *"I am the Alpha and the Omega, the First and the Last, the Beginning and the End"* (Revelation 22: 13).

God is the only one who knows you inside and outside.

> *"[1]O LORD, You have searched me and known me. [2]You know when I sit down and when I rise up; [3]You understand my thought from afar. You scrutinize my path and my lying down, And are intimately acquainted with all my ways. [4]Even before there is a word on my tongue, Behold, O LORD,* ***You know it all"*** (Psalm 139:1-4).

Now, if God is the only entity who knows all things, do you need *some amount* of knowing or understanding of yourself or purpose? Must you learn from others who are going in the direction or pursuing the aspirations that you also desire? Of course, yes. Must we bring back a strong imagination on which to build your unique purpose? In the next chapter, I will discuss God's design of our life's purpose to understand why you must pursue it with uttermost devotion and diligence because you can achieve it.

Chapter 4

Discovering Your Purpose and Living It, an Illusion?

Your purpose is a basic understanding you must have before 'you begin living.' Right, I mean so! God created Adam and Eve and told them their purpose. You have a purpose for coming to earth that you must discover so that you can structure what you do with your endowments, time, and other resources in this life. Your purpose meets your human needs when you invest your endowments and time into it.

In this chapter, I will share some insight into your human needs and how your purpose meets those needs. I discuss the nature of your life's purpose, examining why and how sometimes you're demotivated to keep on track. And I will show you why you must be excited about the very nature and characteristics of your life's purpose.

Your Purpose and Human Needs

Dr. Myles Munroe points out the fundamental needs of human beings. He said everyone has a need for a:

i. Sense of purpose (alignment with what God intended).
ii. Sense of value.
iii. Sense of progress.
iv. Sense of significance or to feel significant (a significant contributor to something).
v. Sense of being important (to be noticed for something).
vi. Sense of meaning (people try to find it in something they do - e.g., yoga and religion).
vii. Sense of fulfillment.
viii. Sense of personal power (to have control over a situation).

Looking at Dr. Munroe's list of human needs, I perceive how they can be achieved when one is living within his or her purpose.

Face-to-Face: Purpose Meets Needs

There is a harmonious relationship between your purpose and needs. When you discover and are living it, it makes a way for each one of your human needs to be taken care of.

Applying Munroe's list of human needs, let's get into how the purpose-to-needs connection works:

> *When you discover your purpose and are living it, there is unity between your purpose and your needs. You're not unsettled, discontented, and looking forward to putting together missing pieces to your life or re-aligning a misfit. Your life is on the right track, and opportunities or challenges don't change who you're or your purpose.*
>
> *Precisely, you feel that your life is meaningful. You're contributing to the universe, so you feel fulfilled. You bring value to others, so you receive pay or reward (more value) for the value you bring to meet the needs of others within your purpose. Progress is evident in your life. People notice you; they see your contributions because, without you, they notice something of value is missing. This is not because you're loud (being loud has*

it is time and value), but because you bring something unique to that gathering and project that no one else can. You're skilled at what you do. You have mastery of various aspects of your life. You have control over yourself because you can, for example, make decisions directed by godly values – you have personal power. You see opportunities today and in the future that fit within your discovered purpose.

Therefore, the unity between your activities, purpose and human needs are intact. These sum up how your human needs are met when you live within your life's purpose.

Given that there is a complete fit between your needs and your purpose, there must be the same between how you're hard-wired and various aspects of life and relationships that you transact with such as work, spouse, and mentor. Good harmony in all the aspects and relationships nourishes your purpose and settles your needs.

As I take stock of my life and the lives of many others that I personally know, I realize how we can wallow around life and hardly look on the inside for what God has deposited for our blessed life. In one workshop I attended, I learned that when human resource professionals advertise a job and call for interviews, what they are looking for is a *suitable* person, not a *fit*. There is a perception in this profession that a fit is impossible.

Nevertheless, I believe that it is possible to have a fit of career, spouse, hobbies, and anything else. And it is not too late to discover your purpose and apply yourself to that activity, work, marriage, or hobby that fits you?

And if you're young and starting to think through your life's purpose or receiving suggestive ideas that are unsettling, you're not alone. Reflect on the possibilities that await you, if you change things around (living how God intended).

- ***Would you rather keep doing the same old things that you've been doing which is getting you nowhere?***

- ***Or would you do something different that works to put you on the right path that your heart is longing for?***

Discovering your purpose and living it allow you to meet your human needs. You align yourself to things that fit you and you become a good fit for the things that align with your purpose, bringing natural harmony to your life. Is that not what we long for? Yes.

God has a plan (i.e., blueprint) for us. These are plans to prosper and bring us to a successful end (Jeremiah 29: 11). In the next segment, I explore the nature of this blueprint, which is also your purpose, and why it appears hidden or looks as if you can never find it.

Is Your Life's Purpose Hidden or an Illusion?

What you discover, you can confront. You must discover your purpose, work on it and live it. And you don't stop living it while you have breath in your lungs. No wonder your life's purpose appears hidden or elusive.

To know your purpose is a solemn necessary discovery process of which you make choices that fit with how God hard-wired you. It is about discovering something that is already in you, but you need 'binoculars.' What do I mean? You need to look inside yourself carefully and prayerfully to see and understand the length, height, breadth, and depth of your gifts and talents and other resources. ***Those who do and follow through with fitting actions reveal God's divine excellence to the world.***

Interestingly, God will sometimes hide such important knowledge from us. There are things we must discover by searching to understand to act on them accordingly. When we discover and understand, then we can explain our lives in meaningful ways – ways that are meaningful to us. We can't explain well what we did not search to discover. The book of Proverbs makes a fascinating point:

> *"It is the glory of God to conceal things, but the glory of kings is to search things out"* (Proverbs 25:2).

You can't confront what you have not identified or discovered. So, people of influence such as Kings find glory or honour in searching out a matter - seeking to understand. God sees us in Christ as kings. He is treating us as such. It is a privilege to search out your purpose!

- ❖ **Often, discovering and living our purpose looks like a false idea or an illusion because this is not made simple for us and for everyone.**

Not much has been done to create clear simple processes for doing this. As necessary as it is, great thinkers or ministers tend to avoid this subject matter. As a result, many believers and others don't know how to go about it. Moreover, after the failures of some who attempted to live a purposeful life, there is a false conclusion that it is too difficult and perhaps impossible to accomplish.

Therefore, is seeking to discover your purpose like chasing the wind and never catching it? Is it a false idea or an illusion? Not at all. We know that even though precious metals (i.e., endowments which make up your purpose) are hidden deep down in the ground, they can be searched for, discovered, and mined when you apply skill and hard work.

- ***Another reason that discovering and living your purpose appears as a false idea is that typically, we prefer to follow immediate or quick gratification – quick answers, quick results, and quick benefits.***

In this high-speed information and technology era, the expectation is that everything should be quick and efficient. Yet purpose is not one of those things that you pursue, achieve, close the page, and move on. Nonetheless, it is satisfying when you successfully translate small goals, projects and ideas into finished products or results.

When you have poured yourself into an endeavour, soon you look forward to a day when your joy soars as your loved ones, fans and spectators celebrate your accomplishment. You hear words that praise and affirm you and validate your skills. Then, the 'little person' inside of you longs to know whether those ideas and efforts were worth pursuing – because there is this doubt that plays on your mind from time to time checking if you will remain committed to your purpose.

When your efforts have yielded something of value to humanity, your heart is filled with joy. You're inspired to keep exploring and doing 'greater impossibilities' as you hear people acknowledge the value that your efforts are bringing. Receiving this kind of feedback keeps you going in the game, although the passion within drives you more. ***We follow quick wins because they encourage us.***

However, your life's purpose is more than a short-term victory or exploit. The marathon does not end when you reach a certain finish line. Purpose is for a lifetime; *it consists of recurring marathon journeys.* But who wants to remain on a journey that never ends? Who begins a journey knowing well that it is not over yet until he or she 'checks out' of this physical earth?

The thought of this continuity of purpose can scare some to think that it is unachievable – that, it is an illusion. It is not surprising that countless people gave up trying harder because of 'what they thought is a muddy, exhausting, and gigantic monster in front of them called purpose.'

The reality is that no one can attain purpose in one day. You attain your life's purpose in parts, and only if you persevere and are patient, then, it is no longer an illusion.

Therefore, is living your life's purpose harmful because it does not end while we are alive? Let's look closer into God's design of life's purpose; God knows what's best for us.

Purpose Never Ends: Is It a Blessing or Curse?

Continuation of purpose is a necessary virtue for keeping us going while we have breath in our lungs. Assuming you can complete life in 10 years from the day you were born, what would you do with the remaining chunk of your time? An idle hand is the devil's workshop. ***God knows that working on your purpose continuously is a source of motivation for your living.***

I recall in March 2020, when the COVID-19 pandemic led to lock-down around the world. The tasks that needed to be completed daily, such as errands and recreational activities outside the home, all ceased. Many had fewer things to do, with plenty of time on their hands since they saved time from hardly riding on the bus, driving to work, or walking to the bus stop to wait for public transportation.

For some, just knowing that they had a few things to do in the day was a reason to procrastinate. Perhaps they wanted to spread their tasks throughout the day or do them later to beat boredom. Everyone copes differently. Your uniqueness is evident here. Certainly, having to pursue your life's purpose day-by-day endlessly while alive, is a blessing in disguise.

Your purpose is a seed that is to be planted, watered, and given the right environment (sunshine) so that it germinates and grows into maturity, and produces fruits. The fruits from your purpose (i.e., nurtured and developed) also contain a seed. The apple tree produces apples, and in the apples are seeds that are planted to yield more apples. The fruit that comes out of your life creates new seeds that you can plant.

So, you see, you never run out of passions, interests, and new projects when you start living within your purpose. In Genesis 8: 22, God confirms that:

> *"While the earth remains, seedtime and harvest, cold and heat, summer and winter, day and night, shall not cease."*

This verse speaks about the period following the floods, which destroyed the entire earth during the time of Noah. God promised never to destroy the earth with a flood. Then He added that man will always enjoy seedtime and harvest time. In other words, there will be continuity of seeding and harvesting while alive.

This continuity of purpose serves some well. Those who appreciate it see it as a chance to get even better at what they do, and to enjoy all the new opportunities that become available - for such there is no room for procrastination.

Others choose to do nothing with their gifts, talents and resources to bring more value because purpose does not end until we leave this earth – they procrastinate because they think they have a lot of time.

- ✓ To live in your purpose is to live as if any day can be your last day on earth.
- ✓ You're only sure of the breath that you have this very moment. You're not sure of your next breath.
- ✓ Do all you can to start living in your purpose today.

We have seen that your purpose could be hidden and appear to be an illusion. What you need is patience and skill to uncover and live it having the awareness that it is an endless privilege and blessing while you have life. To discover and live your purpose, certain fundamental questions are key. Let's explore them in the next chapter.

Chapter 5

Fundamental Questions That Birth Your Life's Purpose

Your purpose is God's intention or reason for our (everyone's) coming to earth. You must answer certain key questions before you will effectively discover your own specific purpose (your practical use), which flows from your understanding of those fundamental questions of life. In this chapter, I will tackle these four fundamental questions: ***Where are am I from? Where am I going? Who are am I? Why am I here?*** – they all shape the reason for your existence as an individual or your specific use. Further in the chapter, I differentiate God's grand purpose for humanity (reason for everyone's existence) from your specific individual purpose (your own practical use on earth).

The Fundamental Questions

Before thinking through why you're on earth, which speaks to your purpose, you must first be clear about **three other fundamental things**:

1. *Where am I from?*
2. *Where am I going?*
3. *Who am I?*

We will tackle these three questions first.

1. Where am I from? You're from God: *"So God created man in His own image; in the image of God, He created him; male and female He created them"* (Genesis 1:27). God made you. He made you like Himself. You're a citizen of heaven where God dwells.

2. Where am I going? You're going to God; you will return to God one day:

- When you accept Christ as your Lord and saviour and remain obedient to His word before your death.
- When Jesus takes you to heaven in the rapture (Jesus comes and takes away His own) so that the

obedient children of God don't experience the suffering, after the rapture.

1 Thessalonians 4:16 assures us:

> *"For the LORD himself will come down from heaven, with a loud command, with the voice of the archangel and with the trumpet call of God, and the dead in Christ will rise first."*

Therefore, salvation must be your priority. Salvation is making Christ the Lord and Saviour of your life by surrendering your life over to Christ Jesus (Romans 10: 9). You accept the sacrifice of Christ's death on the cross so that your sins are forgiven. In Ephesians 1:7, we understand:

> *"In him we have redemption through his blood, the forgiveness of sins, in accordance with the riches of God's grace"*

This sets you up on the path to heaven if you accept Christ and confess Him as the Lord over your life.

> *"If you declare with your mouth, "Jesus is Lord," and believe in your heart that God raised him from the dead, you will be saved"* (Romans 10:9).

Receive Jesus: Simply, you can receive Jesus into your heart and become a born-again believer and follower from this very moment.

If you wish to be born-again and become a follower of Jesus Christ, pray this after me:

> **"Dear Jesus, I make you the Lord of my life. I believe that you died on the cross for my sins. Forgive me of my sins. I promise to love you for the rest of my life. So, help me God...in Jesus' name. Amen!"**

If you prayed this prayer sincerely, congratulations! You're now a new person in Christ. Heaven is rejoicing because your soul is recorded in the book of those slated for heaven. You're blessed.

Next steps:

- ✓ Get a Bible and start reading it. Ask the Holy Spirit to teach you and reveal Christ to you as you study.
- ✓ Find yourself a Bible-believing church to grow in your faith.

Once again, congratulations!

Let's continue reading. The next question before discovering your purpose is:

3. ***Who am I?*** Your identity is in Christ. In Christ, you're being improved or perfected continuously, and your life brings glory to God. 1 Peter 2:9, says in Christ we are a royal priesthood. And Revelation 1:6 affirms that "He [Christ] has made us kings and priests to His God and Father, to Him be glory and dominion forever and ever. Amen." It adds: "... [Christ] has made us kings and priests to His God and Father...." He is also working in us to perfect us in His love.

Moreover, in Christ, you're in a process of continuous transformation and improvement occurring inside and outside because you look to Christ and are enabled by His love. You're transformed from glory to glory as you look unto Jesus Christ.

> *"But we all, with open face beholding as in a glass the glory of the Lord, are changed into the same image from glory to glory [ever-increasing glory], even as by the Spirit of the Lord [which comes from the Lord, who is the Spirit]"* (2 Corinthians 3:18).

You can't be in (and with) Jesus Christ, experience His glory and presence and remain the same.

The glory of the Lord (who is also the Christ) is the power of God that Moses experienced in the Old Testament. This power was so much that the people couldn't look in Moses' face whenever he returned from his fellowship with God. The people had to cover their faces when receiving him (Moses).

But this is no longer necessary for us in the New Covenant. Today, the glory of God is no longer fearful. This is because Christ went back to the Father and sent to us the Holy Spirit. Due to this act, every believer can have the Holy Spirit working in, with and on him daily to bring him closer to God.

Your transformation from glory to glory is the job of the Holy Spirit. It is one thing He does so well. The Holy Spirit is the one who transforms you from one level of glory to another and unto ever-increasing glory. This means that it is impossible to have the Holy Spirit (which is also called the light, wisdom, and power of God) in you and you remain the same.

You're missing something if you experience the Holy Spirit without continuous improvement in character and increasing alignment of your desires with God's grand purpose. What could be preventing the desired transformation or improvement? Discover more hidden secrets about your purpose while you get help to support you.

We see here that understanding your 1. origin, 2. destination and 3. identity - are important for discovering your purpose on earth. In the next section, we look at the final question: **why are you here**? - speaking generally to the grand responsibility that God has given to all of humanity.

God's Grand Purpose for Humanity

God's purpose for all – man and woman – is His intention of your practical use on earth. God prepared you before sending you to earth to ensure that you live your purpose. You're not a biological mistake. You're a sojourner on an assignment accompanied by the resources, authority, and power to carry out a spectacular purpose, which establishes your influence over all things that God created.

You're not a biological accident. How you arrived on earth does not matter – whether you were born into a broken or disjoined home, from unintended pregnancy or by a well-planned pregnancy. God placed you on earth for His glory. If you think that God was so exhausted and threw down a soul, which landed in a shell (body) and womb through the act of sexual intimacy (between your parents) or by artificial insemination (thanks to God for the medical advancements), you're making a mistake. God was not reckless about your soul. He had a plan for you before your soul entered a body to mature and be born. God confirmed His thoughtfulness towards human creation when He spoke to Jeremiah:

> *"Before I formed you in the womb I knew you; Before you were born I sanctified you; I ordained you a prophet to the nations"* (Jeremiah 1:5).

God doesn't make mistakes; He has a purpose and a plan for you before your birth.

Your purpose is to live out God's plan. You did not show up on earth without a plan or a blueprint. There is a plan for you to contribute to life's enrichment. You take away from this earth (e.g., oxygen, food from plants and animals, parent's nourishment, and teacher's knowledge) and you replenish the earth by giving back carbon dioxide (that you exhale or breathe out) in the form of care, innovations, skills, and talents that serve humanity.

God gave humanity (you and I) a grand purpose. Here it is:

> "*And God blessed them, and God said unto them, Be fruitful, and multiply, and replenish the earth, and subdue it: and have dominion over the fish of the sea, and over the fowl of the air, and over every living thing that moveth upon the earth*" (Genesis 1:28).

From this verse, we see that God gave humanity a grand purpose that is in **two parts:**

1. ***Be fruitful, multiply and replenish the earth.***
2. ***Subdue or govern all things (created) on the earth.***

Let's discuss each of them:

Part 1: God's grand purpose for humanity is to 'Be fruitful, multiply and replenish the earth.'

You're here to be fruitful and multiply, and when you do these the earth is replenished. Being fruitful is working towards something God has placed in you. Merriam Webster defines *fruitful*: *involves yielding or producing fruit or being abundantly productive in whatever you do.*

To be fruitful, you need fertile soil for planting, which is **YOU!** Have you ever thought of yourself as fertile or fruitful soil?

You may be living in denial of this truth when you think, 'how can I be fruitful; I'm not a fertile soil'? You say:

- I don't have the right education.
- I did not have the greatest upbringing.
- I am not well-connected to people of influence.

The truth about what God intended for you rules out all factual excuses. These are excuses based on the facts about you and the world in which you live. But these are not your reality.

Next, you multiply when you're fruitful; God wants you to multiply. Merriam Webster Dictionary defines multiply as: "*To increase in number especially greatly or in multiples.*" You multiply in the sense that you produce your kind biologically. God has instructed you to multiply and fill the earth, which means procreating or reproducing children to fill the earth. This is the common meaning often linked to multiplying.

- ***Have you thought of multiplying yourself (socially) by developing others, imparting yourself into others to create unique skill sets?***

- ***Do you realize that multiplying also means 'training new leaders, musicians, computer geeks, electricians, research experts, clergies, horticulturalists, athletes, businesspeople, other tradespeople, and professionals who will add on value and continue your work'***?

You're here to multiply means: you and I are here to continue multiplying great inventions, ideas, money, infrastructure, and handing a better world to generations unborn.

Multiplying is about building a legacy that reproduces and replenishes the earth since we don't last forever on this physical earth.

- ***You're a gift to the earth, but also, you're a gift who keeps on giving back to others and keeps multiplying.***

The result of continuously being fruitful and multiplying is that it replenishes (i.e., *builds up again and fills*: Merriam-Webster Dictionary) the earth. It is a circuit that is not broken and that's why the earth will be replenished. Being fruitful, multiplying, and replenishing form one part of the two-split grand purpose that God set for you (humanity) to live.

Let's look at the second part of God's grand purpose.

Part 2: God's grand purpose for humanity is to 'Subdue or govern.'

You're here to subdue or govern the earth according to Genesis 1: 28. To govern means, you lead the affairs of the earth and make decisions on jurisdictions and things for which you're accountable. In nations that practice democracy, elected and appointed officials make decisions on behalf of the citizens. And the ruling government is accountable for the well-being of the citizenry.

In God's system, ***you're here to govern or subdue,*** which means you have considerable autonomy, with the word of God and Holy Spirit, when you do. To subdue is to bring all things under your authority so that the earth obeys your commands and wishes. You're the driver of all affairs of any part of the earth because God has given you power and authority to rule over or have dominion over all things and people. Unfortunately, some Christians are experiencing this dominion. Those who are living their purpose can testify that dominion is key to living your life's purpose. Do you have this dominion attitude, or are you stepping into it now?

Adam and Eve lost their dominion in the Garden of Eden by giving in to the temptation of the serpent, Satan. However, God restored this dominion to us through the blood of Jesus Christ (in the New Covenant). We are no longer slaves to sin and Satan. Fearing and serving God in your surrendered life guarantees you power and authority from the Holy Spirit; this makes all things submit to you.

> *"Behold, I give unto you power [authority] to tread on serpents and scorpions, and over all the power [authority] of the enemy: and nothing shall by any means hurt you"* (Luke 10:19).

You must have dominion over all things God created on the earth. This is part of the two-split grand purpose God set for you.

What principles will make you dominate, subdue, be fruitful, multiply and replenish the earth?

Let's explore this. God's grand purpose for you will occur if you're living for Christ and apply knowledge, faith, obedience to the word, and the Holy Spirit diligently. For example, how do you dominate? You dominate by influence; by the obedience to God and adherence to His guidance through the word. With this, the Holy Spirit will make a way for you to bring value and gather influence. This, in turn, opens doors to opportunities to bring value, more resources and greater influence. Apostle Paul says:

> *"Therefore let no one boast in men. For all things are yours"* (1 Corinthians 3:21).

We know that God's proclamation of your purpose in Genesis 1:28 says, you're to be fruitful, multiply and have dominion over all things.

And practically, this is how it occurs:

1. When you use your gifts to provide a solution to the king's need or a problem, this brings value to the king.
2. It opens doors to bringing in wealth, (i.e., you have fruits and are multiplying) and to greater wealth.
3. The value you produce brings influence. With influence comes dominion and more dominion.

> *"A man's gift [given in love or courtesy] makes room for him and brings him before great men [kings]"* (Proverbs 18:16).

It is important to choose to live in Christ to secure a blessed outcome. Otherwise, God's reason for sending you to earth will be diverted into painful, unfulfilling, and eventually, a wasted life.

> "*You say, 'I am rich. I have everything I want. I do not need a thing!' And you do not realize that you are*

> *wretched and miserable and poor and blind and naked"* (Revelations 3:17).

Don't be deceived when some family members, friends, distant acquaintances, or successful people give the impression that you can have a fulfilling life without Christ. There is such proof in places like Hollywood, Wall Street, and among members of your community. You may therefore be tempted to think or feel:

- *Why should I live God's purpose for humanity with Christ at the center, if some have blissful lives without God?*

The truth is this: To be living a kind of purposeful life outside of Christly principles is no purpose; it is a big loss to you, humanity, and heaven. No amount of money, fame or luxury must replace Christ in your life. You're here on earth to have the life you desire while following the way of Christ in love.

Likewise, you're fruitful in all you do when you remain in Christ.

> *"Remain in me, as I also remain in you. No branch can bear fruit by itself; it must remain in the vine. Neither*

> *can you bear fruit unless you remain in me"* (John 15:4).

We have seen that understanding why we are here, our grand purpose, is an awareness that reveals God's intention for you (humanity) to increase and rule over the affairs of creation and all that is in it. This is a reality that encourages and empowers you to increase your influence and dominion. It also means that this quest must be guided by Godly principles. Understanding this and the other fundamental questions is the foundation from which you can determine your specific purpose; your small piece of the big pie that you do to attain God's grand purpose for humanity. In the next section, we will look at the nature of this specific purpose and what it must accomplish.

What is Your Specific Purpose?

Your specific purpose is the reason you exist or your practical use (that God determined before you were born), which ultimately will improve others and your life. Your specific purpose is accompanied by gifts and talents that will help you to achieve it. Freed Dictionary defines purpose as:

> *"1. the reason for which anything is done, created, or exists. 2. a fixed design, outcome, or idea that is the object of an action or other effort. 3. fixed intention in doing something; determination: a man of purpose. 4. practical advantage or use: to work to good purpose."*

Since God's grand purpose for you is the reason for being on earth, you must think in terms of purpose.

To think in <u>terms of your specific purpose</u> is to:

1. ***Act on your practical use.***
2. ***Provide solutions to challenges or problems.***
3. ***Add value to life and the earth.***

God's grand purpose for all – men and women – is his intention of our reason for existence or use here on earth. But you have a specific unique purpose within this grand purpose.

In Genesis 1: 26,

> *Then God said, "Let us make mankind in our image, in our likeness, so that they may rule over the fish in the sea and the birds in the sky, over the livestock and all*

> *the wild animals, and over all the creatures that move along the ground."*

God loudly spoke His intention while He was yet to create man.

Then, after God made male and female (man and woman), He took the time to inform them of their purpose. God *told them their purpose* so that they don't go about doing something else that He didn't intend for them to do.

Again, see what God said to them:

> *"Be fruitful, and multiply, and replenish the earth, and subdue it: and have dominion over the fish of the sea, and over the fowl of the air, and over every living thing that moveth upon the earth"* (Genesis 1:28).

God's intentions apply to you - both man and woman. The word 'man' is used here as universal, to mean ***all people***. So, you're only **one** (***one man***) of **all people**.

While God's purpose for you is to be fruitful, multiply, replenish, govern, or subdue the earth, you're only '**one man**.' I mean you can only do your part or piece.

- Therefore, ***what is your piece that you will do to contribute to achieving God's grand purpose (big pie) for humankind?***

If you answer this question, then, you know your specific purpose. As you think about your specific purpose, I want you to think about the following questions:

1. What has God put in you that needs to come out and be a blessing to humanity? That's your purpose.
2. What do you do (or can do) that makes you so excited, which is a solution to a problem or someone's need? That's your purpose.
3. What is a burning desire in your heart that you will die for? That's your purpose.
4. What do you enjoy and do with significant ease, no matter its difficulty for others? That's your purpose.
5. What do you have in you that could be developed even more to meet a need or be a solution to a problem? That's your purpose.

A person's specific purpose is not always obvious. Your purpose is to be discovered so that you can pursue it. Prophet Jeremiah in the Bible didn't know his purpose until that remarkable day God spoke to him and said:

> *"Before I formed you in the womb, I knew you, and before you were born, I set you apart and appointed you as a prophet to the nations"* (Jeremiah 1: 5).

God called Jeremiah to be His prophet or mouthpiece. He was to deliver God's message to him to the intended audience - nation and people – to warn and guide them to reconcile with God. But it was not until God visited him in a vision (i.e., a spiritual encounter with God where he received messages while fully awake) that he knew what he was born to do or his practical use. God had a need or problem that Jeremiah will meet or solve. Jeremiah wouldn't have known his specific purpose if not because of this vision.

- ***Does God always initiate the move to show us our specific purpose as he did with Jeremiah? Something to think about.***

Your specific purpose is your contribution to God's grand purpose to increase (be fruitful, multiply and replenish the earth) and influence or impact (have dominion over) all He created. **Your specific purpose calls on your talents, passions, skills, and experiences to solve a problem, meet a need, or add value to life or humanity.** We must take the initiative to search to discover that specific purpose. God can reveal to you as you search it. In the next chapter, let's get into the easy steps to discover your specific purpose.

Chapter 6

Steps to Discover Your Specific Purpose

We saw in the previous chapters that the reasons people are unable to discover their specific purpose, let alone live it, are to an extent, connected to their little to no understanding of their purpose. Often, you don't have adequate, clear, practical instructions to guide you to discover it. ***The process of discovering your specific purpose is adventurous, exciting, and rewarding, given the positively pleasant impact that a discovered purpose will have on your day-to-day satisfaction.***

In this chapter, first, I will introduce you to a broad and simple step-by-step process of unveiling your specific purpose from within. Secondly, I will walk you through step 1 to identify your key resources or assets within you that shape your purpose. I will show you how to use templates/worksheets in the book to make the process simpler for you. I will explain the remaining steps in the following two chapters (7 and 8).

Highlights of Steps to Discover Your Purpose

To discover your purpose, I walk you through the following 8 steps:

1. **Identify your Abilities, Potentials, Passions, and Pains (APPP):** This is a self-inquiry process to list these resources in you that make you want to do one thing and not the other.
2. **Identify the general impacts of doing something about your passions**: Briefly explain the impact your individual passion(s) could have (on a. *others* and b. *yourself*), should you do something about them. For example, to intervene with a solution, project, or program.
3. **Identify and explain the reason(s) for your pains**: Briefly explain the reasons for each of your pain points (matters that frustrate, anger you or cause displeasure).

4. **Create a Purpose Statement** (PS): Use the information you've gathered about your key resources –APPP – to create a Purpose Statement to show their logical connections.
5. **Identify activities/activity themes matching your APPP**: Select activities/activity themes that you desire to do that match with your identified abilities, potential, passions, and pains – APPP. There are several things you can do.
6. **Identify and explain how your selected activities and activity themes improve (impact) lives**: Briefly explain how the activities you've identified based on your APPP could improve the lives of others as well as impact your own life.
7. **Create a *Picture* Purpose Statement (PPS)**: Create a visual form of your Purpose Statement in step 4. Include the *potential impacts on others and yourself* of the activities/activity themes you've listed in step 6.
8. **Create a Detailed Picture Purpose (DPP)**: Add your list of activity/activities themes you would like to carry out to the Picture Purpose

you created in step 7; this becomes your (DPP) – *this is also your discovered purpose.* See Figure 4, Life's Purpose Discovery Cycle, page 144.

Now, let's go into the details of the *8 steps*. The first is to identify the resources that God has given to you as you arrived on earth.

What Are the Key Resources that God Put in You?

Everything pertaining to life was already given to you when you arrived on earth. God did not create you and place you on earth without the gifts, talents, and physical resources that you need to survive and thrive. It is not in the nature of God to plant a fruit tree before thinking about what kind of fruit it can bear. God was systematic, methodical or very thoughtful in His creation. The land was made before the trees and plants. God did not get to the middle of creation before imagining what is possible. He has generously endowed each one with gifts and talents.

The Christian and non-Christian have gifts and talents because we are all God's creation. But by receiving Christ, you receive a new spirit (the Holy Spirit), which becomes part of the gifts and talents you possess. According to Dr. Myles Munroe,

> *"Everything you were born to become is trapped in yourself; you are loaded.... Whatever you were born to be and to do is already in you. Your future is not ahead of you, your future is trapped inside you. You came to the planet earth with your future inside you."*

To illustrate how we sometimes doubt our abilities, let's examine Jeremiah again. God clearly told him that He was to be a prophet, meaning he will know God's mind and speak it (as His mouthpiece) to the people. A prophet is a person ordained by God to give direction for cleansing, to pray for the people, and to lead. When God called Jeremiah, He told him his specific assignment or purpose.

Jeremiah doubted if he had the skills to carry out this assignment. He did by pointing out his deficiencies:

> *"Ah, Lord GOD,"* .... *"I surely do not know how to speak, for I am only a child!"* (Jeremiah 1: 6).

God assured him that not only will He be with him, but also that He has provided whatever he needed to succeed, so he must not worry.

> *"Then the LORD reached out His hand, touched my mouth, and said to me: "Behold, I have put My words in your mouth"* (Jeremiah 1:9).

God called Jeremiah at a young age, as a teenager or even younger as indicated by diverse accounts. When he worried that he had poor speech, he didn't know the resources that God had prepared for that specific assignment or purpose.

> ***There are gifts and talents that we have as part of our biological make-up from birth. We grow in our gifts and talents as we work with them, use them, or learn more about them.***

For example, the more you use or learn a particular skill or subject, the more knowledgeable you become. You gain greater expertise, and you become a master in that field over time.

However, your sharpness in a specific field of study or subject is because of how God has hard-wired you for your specific assignment. For example, you don't know why you love mathematics – in other words, God has hard-wired the love for calculations in you. Later in life, you find out that you're not a fan of learning languages. However, you found that being skilled in one or more languages such as English language, Afrikaans, French or Spanish is a must for getting into postsecondary to further your education in mathematics. Your college instructors and university professors understand that you need speaking and writing fluency in a formal language to be able to complete your mathematics studies at a higher level.

Also, they believe that your mathematical skills will be more useful in solving real-world problems if you can communicate formally in them. So, you did your best to succeed in one of those languages. But you scored extremely higher grades in mathematics and related subjects. **Hence, your tendency to love certain subjects is a gift for your specific purpose.**

The Bible talks about various ***spiritual gifts*** that are available to you (the believer in Christ) and these are:

1. Gift of mercy, teaching, serving, leading, encouraging, giving, and prophesying (Romans 12:6-8).
2. Gift of being apostles, prophets, evangelists, pastors, and teachers (Ephesians 4: 11-12).
3. Gift of preaching (I Peter 4: 10-11).
4. Gifts of word of wisdom, word of knowledge, faith, healing, miraculous powers, prophecy, distinguishing between spirits, speaking in different kinds of tongues and interpretation of tongues (1 Corinthians 12: 7-10).
5. Gifts of working as apostles, prophets, teachers, working of miracles, and gifts of healing, of helping, of guidance, and of different kinds of tongues (1 Corinthians 12: 28).

You receive these gifts in various ways. Apostle Paul points that you can have a gift by deeply desiring it (1 Corinthians 14:39). Also, you receive these gifts by attaining certain levels of maturity in your obedience and faithfulness (Acts 5:32). And by the working or exercising the power of the Holy Spirit within (Ephesians 3:20) and people laying hands on you to transmit a gift(s) they have to you (2 Timothy 1:6).

Imagine this: Since the *spiritual gifts alone* given to believers is this extensive, think about the gifts, talents, potentials, and passions available to *everyone* (or anyone) for thriving and improving on life.

Since Adam and Eve lost their privilege of dwelling in the presence of God forever, we have had to be more involved in organizing our livelihoods. I think of the multitude of biological (or physiological) gifts and talents (e.g., brainpower, muscle power, eloquence, and others) that God has given to us. Everyone uses his or her resources within (endowments) in producing and distributing goods and services in one or more of these areas:

> *Cultivating crops, transportation (air, land, and sea), defence, public service, curing of sicknesses, business, building homes, office buildings and public facilities, mining, manufacturing, banking, and animal husbandry.*

For example, will all these sectors work well if we all have the same biological resources within us? ***We apply the biological gifts together with our different spiritual gifts in working with the natural environment***

(e.g., rain, sun, land, plants, sea, water, and animals) to survive and thrive. The kinds of resources we possess dictate how we use them. I also call these groups of resources your backbone.

Next, let's look at the nature of the individual groups of resources in you, which you must identify to help to discover your purpose.

Resources in YOU: Abilities, Potentials, Passions, and Pains (APPP)

God has placed in each one of us certain desires, ambitions, and dispositions of which some are shaped by our experiences in this world. In other words, certain traits, interests, and experiences point you to your purpose. They are your resources or backbone that steer your purpose. Dr. Myles Munroe called them ***SEEDS.***

According to him:

- ✓ **The seed of a thing is in itself.**
- ✓ **The end of a thing is hidden in the thing.**
- ✓ **Everything a thing is to become is in itself.**
- ✓ **God placed the future of a thing in itself.**

Everyone possesses these seeds as gifts. In other words, what you will become in this life is already in you in seed form. Therefore, the seeds must be nurtured in the right environment to grow into a tree and produce fruits.

The 'seeds' inside are your ***Abilities, Potentials, Passions, and Pains (APPP or AP^3)*** that determine your purpose.

Abilities

Your *abilities* are one of your key resources in life. Merriam Webster Dictionary defines abilities as the natural talent or acquired competency or skills in doing something. ***Abilities are what you already have and what you're known for. You may have built a level of mastery in such things.*** It could be something for which you have acquired skills by studying, apprenticing, practicing and through coaching. You may be skilled in computer programing, designing structures, delivering babies, accounting, nursing the sick, developing websites and using social media. These are abilities you might have trained for to attain the mastery that you have.

Potentials

Another resource you have is *potential.* Potential, according to Merriam Webster Dictionary, is something that can develop or can become actual. Potential exists as possibilities, which can develop into an actual form. Potentials are assets in you that are not fully developed or explored. ***Potential refers to what you have that can be developed into something increasingly useful or beneficial.***

Potential is usually within a developmental process of formation because it still needs more exploration, more exercise, and more practice to produce or materialize the possibilities in it.

For example, you may have the potential to become a journalist:

- If you're good with understanding ideas.
- If you can guide a conversation among small or large groups.
- If you can ask insightful questions and you can communicate clearly with ease.

These potentials are gifts God has given to you, of which you can develop, train, learn more about or use more for it to grow.

Passion

Passion is another form of resource, which points you to your purpose. Merriam Webster Dictionary defines ***passion as an intense drive, desire, conviction, ardent affection, deep interest, a strong liking, or devotion to something.*** To have passion for something is to be consumed by it in thought and at heart, leading to your devotion to it. This thing could be an idea, a concept, an activity, or an object.

When you're passionate about something, you're willing to sacrifice to see it to fruition, to become a finished product and to see it manifest fully. There is a feeling of happiness, excitement, pleasure, and satisfaction when you think about it or when you do those things about which you're passionate. The thought about what you're passionate about gets you inspired to do something more.

> *Some people have the passion to help, give, repair broken items, and heal the sick or prevent sickness. I have*

heard people say to me, I hate injustice, so I want the right thing to be done. Such people will be the first to call the TV or radio station to report an incident and to write letters to the President to address a situation. Their desire is to prevent wrong, fix wrong and ensure more right happens in society.

- ***Passion drives abilities and potentials; it is the engine that moves your abilities and potentials.***

While your passion could be in your DNA, which is a part of God's creation in you, you may pick up new passions along the way in life as you experience different situations – both good and bad. Each passion you develop in life relies on the fundamental gifts, dispositions, or tendencies already in you. This explains why you love to do one thing and not the other. But you could face an interesting situation.

TWO things about the PASSION:

1. ZERO PASSION (or Passion problem): This is where you have gifts and talents (abilities and potentials), but you don't have the passion to put

them to use. Passion drives talents and gifts (abilities).

2. ZERO TALENT (or Talent problem): This is where you have a passion for something, but you don't have the gifts and talents (abilities) to live the passion. Gifts and talents don't drive themselves. They need passion to thrive.

Pains

The pains within us are another source that guides our purpose. ***Our pains refer to the points of displeasure in a person's life, which provoke tough or unpleasant emotions such as frustration, hurt and anger***. Our experiences of pain and displeasure lead us to a discovery of new passion. And these make you *happy, excited, and satisfied – they inspire* you.

❖ Pains are situations that upset you, frustrate or annoy you, creating unhappiness or displeasure in you.

An example is this:

You may have a passion to end poverty because you experienced child poverty growing up. You struggled to pay your way through school and endured hunger sometimes. You walked over 6 to 8 km to school and back because you only had sufficient funds to buy food and nothing else.

These experiences could create in you a passion for projects to support the education of poor children to get through school and to build careers that will eventually end child poverty. You may not have come into this world with a passion for education, but your lived experiences have spurred in you a passion to assist poor children in their educational pursuits.

Moreover, any unpleasant experience can lead you to a new passion. It could be a miscarriage; loss of a child, sibling, or marriage; chronic sickness; drug and alcohol addiction; or political crisis. These events can create in you a passion for prenatal care, midwifery (doula/birthing coach), counselling, public health education, health research, gift of healing, working of miracles and leadership in politics. Positive experiences can also lead to new passions such as excelling in school, sports, raising funds for a worthy cause or being lauded for a creative project at work.

Table 1: Sample of your abilities, potentials, passions, and pains (APPP or AP^3 list)

Abilities	Potentials	Passions	Pains
Computer programming	Wisdom	Learning & growing	Physical pain
Leadership	Sickness prevention	Business	Poverty
Organizing	Healing	Healthy eating	Rape
Marketing	Writing	Running	Sickness
Performance improvement	Teaching	Journaling	Conflicts
Training/teaching	Business	Volunteering	Motor vehicle accident
Sports	Basketball	Weight control	Loss of employment
Researching	Preaching	Inspiring others	Grief
Counselling	Making people laugh	Crocheting/ knitting	Addiction

Abilities	**Potentials**	**Passions**	**Pains**
Swimming	Restoring machines	Teaching	Juvenile children
Decluttering	Interior design	Dancing	Wasting time
Physical body training	Mechanical engineering	Advising	Suicide
Security/defence	Opera singing	Helping people	Anxiety/worry
Crafts	Clothing design & sewing	Politics	Surgery
Computer programming	Art	Gardening	Theft
Drawing structures	Healing	Intercession	Abuse
Caring for animals	Driving	Raising funds for charity	Abduction
Defense	Agriculture	Fixing machines	Gang violence
Swimming	Social media presence	Evangelizing	Divorce

Abilities	**Potentials**	**Passions**	**Pains**
Caring for animals	Learning a new language	Personal hygiene	Disability
Drawing structures	Playing instruments	Organizing	Physical pain
Computer programming	Electronics	Working around nature	Prison
Decluttering	Animal care	Chatting on-line	Mental disorder
Physical body training	Nursing	Reading	Debt

In the next section, I will walk you through how to self-assess to identify the specific abilities, potentials, passions, and pains (APPP or AP^3) that you have. These are the resources that will help you to determine your specific purpose in life.

Get to Know Your Abilities, Potentials, Passions, and Pains (APPP)

Now, you know that God has given you resources and your life experiences also shape the resources that you use. What you do from here is to set aside time and energy to self-assess to identify your resources or backbone.

- ***Your backbone holds you together. It is what carries you around; that is what your APPP does. Ideally, every person can have several of each of the APPP qualities.***

For example, I have a passion for singing, mentoring, and teaching. Also, my abilities include telling stories, research, designing and the list goes on. In a couple of years, I imagine I will have additional abilities and passions as I learn new things and have new experiences. What could they be?

The mistake that people make is to trivialize this APPP or resource discovery process. Today, in human resource circles, employers are aware that what keeps a person in high performance on a job might not be exactly what you're thinking.

Let's Do a Quick Quiz:

Which among the following will you choose as the top three qualities that today's employers look for in a candidate*? Education, personality, skills, experience, motivation, emotional intelligence, attitude, and interest?*

Did you choose: *education, skills, and experience? Surprisingly, those are incorrect*. In today's global society, human resource practitioners are particularly interested in these: ***motivation, personality, and attitude*** *– these are correct.*

The issue is that most job applicants are well educated. Some experts believe that high school graduation is only good enough for getting along. For a decent living, you need more than high school education. This means that skills or education appear irrelevant in selecting one candidate over the other at the interviewing stage. Why?

Most people applying for a particular job most likely have the education and skills required for the job; what differentiates candidates could be their level of motivation, attitude and personality.

You're now wondering: is education no longer important? Are my skills no longer important? With the kind of expectations that employers have now, it is reasonable to say that qualities such as passion and pains are big drivers of one's performance on any task. When a person applies their job-specific abilities (including other skills such as time management, team management, and leadership) to their passions (and passions from pains), you have an employee who is self-driven and a high performer – certainly an interesting, new way of thinking!

- **What are you using your skills for?**
- **Are you using your skills for what gives you joy and satisfies you?**

Discovering your specific purpose will help you to do that more easily. The next thing is to take stock of your *four* resources (i.e., APPP).

Preparing to Take Stock of Your APPP

There are things you must do in preparation to take stock. Preparing a day or two ahead before you take stock will help to make it effective. Setting time with yourself and others to be involved, preparing for the methods, worksheets, notebooks or books, gadgets, and consecration are important preparations.

- ✓ **Set up a convenient time**: Set up a time in the day or night that you're most effective. What you will be doing here is to examine your life to identify the APPP you already have. This is what I call: ***taking stock*** on your own and with others.

- ✓ **Fast and pray:** Since this exercise requires your mind, heart, and soul, ensure that you have peace within all faculties. Consider taking a day or two to fast and pray to fine-tune your ability to flow or to be open to your inner voice and the Holy Spirit before embarking on this exercise. This is helpful for adults (or even young people) who already have so much going on in their lives and must silence the noise or distractions within. Fasting with prayer is generally beneficial for this solemn process of self-discovery.

- ✓ **Prepare to think from buckets**: For those who find it challenging thinking through many things at a time, prepare to analyze your life in compartments or buckets. Then, you will realize that you have covered all the buckets as you put the information together.

An example is thinking of your life in terms of economic, social, physical, spiritual, mental, emotional, environmental, and political buckets. Apply all four areas of the APPP to each of these buckets:

i. **Bucket 1: Economic**
   - What are my economic abilities?
   - What are my economic potentials?
   - What are my economic passions?
   - What are my economic pains?

ii. **Next, bucket 2: Mental**
   - What are my mental abilities?
   - What are my mental potentials?
   - What are my mental passions?
   - What are my mental pains?

You keep doing that until you go through all the buckets.

✓ **Invite trusted others**: Set up time with trusted others to help you in this assessment exercise. Find one or two trusted friends, family members or someone who knows you well, a mentor or coach. You will talk with this person later after you've identified your APPP. You will give them enough time to get back to you with their feedback. The meeting can be in person or virtual. Your goal is to get their candid opinion about your APPP. The reason is that sometimes you're uncertain of your APPP. Discuss your expectations with them prior, so that they will be ready to provide you with helpful insights when you're ready.

Follow these steps to identify your resources or backbone.

Steps to Inquire into Yourself: Taking Stock of Your Resources

1. **Spend ample time as you need**: Spend three to four hours or more (as much as needed) on this discovery process. Avoid distraction. Don't be in a rush. This is about your 'life's purpose' so give it the respect and quality time that it is due.

2. **List your APPP**: Make a list of all your resources – abilities, potentials, passions, and pains - using the APPP sheet in Table 2. Don't be too critical about yourself. Revise your list as much as you need during this period.

    - **Method**: Use the bucket list approach if that will be easier for you. It makes your process and the result more thorough. *You can break each bucket down into small buckets*. See an example here.

    Economic bucket:

    a. What are my **economic** *abilities?* Now, ask small bucket questions on economics, but separately on your *abilities, potentials, passions and pains- APPP*.

    - What are your abilities in **making profits or owning a business**?
    - What are your abilities in **managing your finances**?

b. What are my **economic** *pains?*
   - What are my *pains* in **the stock market?**
   - What are my *pains* in financial management - handling of my credit cards, bills and the like?

   Do the same for all buckets and APPPs.

3. **Meet trusted support**: After you've made your own APPP list, meet with your trusted support to get feedback on your APPP list? Ask for any suggested revisions to your APPP, including anything you missed or misplaced. Do this again with another trusted person if you need more feedback to clarify or validate your thoughts. But don't get stuck; move on with the process as quickly as possible.

4. **Have gratitude all through:** Review your list with a heart of gratitude. Don't try to disagree with your trusted person's comments. Receive feedback with grace and an open

mind; arguing over their opinion can hinder genuine feedback. Be thankful that you get to discover your purpose.

5. **Pray over your completed APPP**: Take some time to pray about your list. Again, add fasting if you can to improve your connection with your inner voice and the Holy Spirit. Whatever you don't have inner peace about, cross it out from your list. Should you be reminded that something is missing, add it to your list. If you feel your list reflects your APPP well, then, you're done. But don't be stuck.

6. **APPP ready for next steps**: You will use your APPP list as the basis for the subsequent phases in the discovery process. This is not a fixed list. You can revise as things change.

Use Table 2 below to fill in your APPP or AP^3

TIP: You can have more than one APPP under each column. Don't worry if you come up with fewer or more resources than you anticipated. What matters is whether you have reasonably emptied your mind and heart onto the worksheet.

Table 2: Ideal Connections within the APPP.

What is my ability?	What is my potential?	What is my passion?	What is my pain?
1.	1.	1.	1.
2.	2.	2.	2.
3	3.	3.	3.
4.	4.	4.	4
5.	5.	5.	5.
6.	6.	6.	6.
Ability: natural talent or acquired skills in doing something you're good at.	**Potential**: something that can develop into an actual form.	**Passion:** intense drive, desire, deep interest and a strong liking or devotion to some activity, object, or concept that excites, satisfies, and inspires you.	**Pain:** a situation that frustrates, upsets, and irritates you, or causes displeasure.

So far, you've seen the first thing to discover your purpose: you carefully take stock of your APPP to know what you have. In the following chapter, I will walk you through how to create connections among the various resources (i.e., APPP) to produce a Purpose Statement.

Chapter 7

Writing Your Purpose Statement

A Purpose Statement broadly guides your decisions through the course of your life. A Purpose Statement gives you and others a quick snapshot of your purpose. According to California's Dominican University psychology professor, Dr. Gail Matthews, those who write down their goals are 42% more likely to achieve them (Castrillon, 2021). Just by writing them down, you have a far greater chance of achieving them than someone who didn't.

Now that you know the constitution of your purpose: abilities, potentials, passions, and pains; with this APPP, you will create your Purpose Statement with the details. In this chapter, I will show you how to create a broad Purpose Statement along with its visual representation that summarizes your purpose.

Steps to Create an Effective Purpose Statement

The first thing in creating your Purpose Statement is to think carefully about your passions. Not only does your passion affect other lives in a positive way when you pursue them; it will bring more value into your life. Your pains also set off your passions. So, it is important to reflect on the reasons why you wish to do something about experiences that have been painful to you.

Now, we will carefully study my list of resources (Table 3) and tease out the key themes to create a Purpose Statement. You can do the same for yourself.

Create a worksheet for your Purpose Statement. Using Table 3 as a guide, do the following:

1. Think about what each passion that you listed will accomplish in people's lives and your own life should you pursue it.
2. Briefly write down how your listed passions will benefit or impact you and others, should you

pursue them. Separate those for you and those for others.

3. Think about your pains or points of displeasure, both past and present listed.

4. Briefly explain why you would like to do something about each pain point listed.

Table 3 below is a working list that I have created for myself. This list is not conclusive.

Table 3: Worksheet for Creating a Purpose Statement

APPP	Input 1	Input 2	Input 3
What are my abilities?	Researching	Teaching/training	Analyzing
What are my potentials?	Singing	Cooking	Encouragement
What are my passions? **What will they do for**	Counselling	Evangelizing	Learning new things & skills

others and yourself?	What will this do for others? *(Gives hope, encouragement, peace, tools, solutions, and skills)* What will this do for me? *(Makes me happy, inspired and is fulfilling)*	What will this do for others? *(Gives hope and brings souls to Christ - salvation)* What will this do for me? *(I feel fulfilled, brings me joy)*	What will these do for others? *(Brings understanding and solutions to meet their life needs)* What will these do for me? *(Makes me knowledgeable, useful and attracts value to me in the form of provision)*
What are my pains?	Sickness Why? *(I've frequently been sick and don't wish others to suffer like I did).*	Wasting time Why? *(Lacking understanding made me waste time with decisions. I want to change that for others)*	Unforgiveness Why? *(People hinder their joy and progress when unable to let go of the hurt. I have freedom in this area, and I want others to be free too)*

In the next section, I discuss how the four APPPs link together to create harmony within the Purpose Statement.

Connect: Your Abilities, Potentials, Passions, and Pains to the Purpose Statement

Now that you have made your list in these four rows, it is time to examine how they connect with one another. In writing your Purpose Statement, focus on your passions first. Think about how they are related to your pains or points of displeasure. One of the items I am passionate about from the list is to learn new things and skills. Also, from my list, one of my pains is sickness.

Since my passion is learning new things and skills, I will love to *learn* about sicknesses and ways to prevent, cure or heal them. You can see that my passion is connected with my pain. There is a natural harmony between my passion and pain if I use my passion for learning new things towards my pain from sickness. This is called **alignment**. You must maximize the unity between these two items.

> *Use your* ***abilities and potentials*** *(gifts and talents) for your* ***passions and pains****. The natural harmony between them brings you motivation and fulfillment.*

For example, I have a passion to sing, but not the talent to take it to the level where I can impact millions. That is not to say that you can't produce anything outstanding from a passion that lacks the matching talents and abilities. If you have a passion to sing, you can take singing lessons to become an outstanding singer. However, the former scenario where passion aligns with abilities, talents and potentials is easier and quicker to attain.

Further, let's look at abilities and potentials closely for connections between them. Your abilities and potentials are part of the resources that you must use to achieve your passion and to tackle your pain. For example, my abilities include research and teaching, whereas my potentials include cooking and singing.

Suppose I follow my passion of counselling, learning new things or skills and evangelizing (i.e., winning souls for Christ) in the list in Table 3, I will be using my researching, analyzing, and teaching abilities to prepare, teach, guide and lead people to Christ, while also guiding them with tools to manage the difficult life situations.

Further, I will use my potential for singing and cooking to serve those I am counselling or ministering to in many ways. I could also teach others to cook and sing if I master the art of doing them. Ideally, you must direct your *abilities* and *potentials* for your *passions* and to intervene in your *pains*.

I have demonstrated the relationship among these four resources (i.e., backbone). Now, let's create my purpose statement of fewer than 100 words. The fewer words the better. See Table 3 with my own list of resources to know how I produced my purpose statement below.

Figure 1: A Purpose Statement

I love to counsel, evangelize, and learn and share new things/skills [Passions & Pains] by researching, teaching/training, analyzing, cooking, and singing [Abilities & Potentials] to **bring peace, hope, salvation, solutions, fulfillment, and health to people's lives [Impact on others],** WHICH CONSEQUENTLY BRINGS ME JOY, FULFILLMENT, AND PROVISION [IMPACT ON MY LIFE].

In this example, my passions are italicized. The benefits (impact) that my passions bring to others are bolded. My abilities and potential are underlined, and finally how my passions personally impact me are in upper case letters.

Create your own Purpose Statement of fewer than 100 words. You will find the time and effort satisfying, given that this is part of the blueprint or map that will guide you to carry out your life's purpose.

Figure 2: Ideal Inter-connections within the APPP

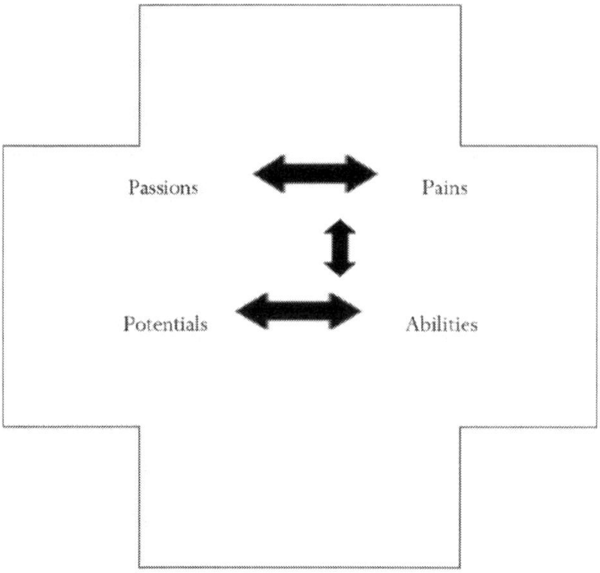

Next, is a discussion of how to handle your Purpose Statement to provide the most benefit.

Is Your Purpose Statement Permanent?

Your purpose statement should not be static; you can revise it periodically, but not frequently. As you saw earlier, your passion can keep changing due to experiences that bring new sources of pain or displeasure, thereby, new projects or programs to address them. As you keep learning and experiencing life, you become better at various things and tasks, and you're likely to pick up new potentials that you can develop further. Therefore, a Purpose Statement is flexible and subject to change when you make new discoveries about yourself.

However, you must avoid revising it too frequently – because if you do so, it will no longer serve as a reference or map. This defeats the purpose of the statement. You can revise perhaps once or twice a year. The intent of revising the Purpose Statement is to capture any major shifts to allow you to refine, add on and drop any existing details as needed.

We have seen how to create your Purpose Statement. A self-inquiry process to identify your APPP is a key resource for your Purpose Statement. With this, you make logical connections among the components of your APPP. In the next chapter, we will look at how to select activities and activity themes that align with your purpose statement, to develop a detailed picture version of your purpose statement.

Chapter 8

Creating Your Detailed Picture Purpose

A ***picture speaks louder than words.*** You can forget words, but you won't forget pictures and how they make you feel. Often, the reason we don't move on our purpose is that we forget it when life gets busy, and challenges and opportunities come. It is important to see a picture of where you're going in life and the activities that you must do to get there. This is a reminder of the key nuts and bolts of your purpose Such images remind us to keep focused. In this chapter, I will guide you, first, to create picture representations of your purpose and second, to create a detailed version of your purpose that contains impact-making activities that you will do to live your purpose well.

In Your Face: Creating a Picture of Your Purpose Statement

Your Purpose Statement (PS) is a broad statement that guides your life's decisions. It does not contain all the details of the decisions that you will be making. But it does serve as the starting point to discover the activities and decisions that are likely to fit the way God hard-wired you.

Aside from your simple broad Purpose Statement, you will include the details by identifying the key activities that will complement or support your Purpose Statement. At this point, it is like creating a map to lead you to the destination that you want to go in your life.

- ***A Purpose Statement that you don't see or don't remember exists or you don't know where it is, should no longer be your guide.***

The mistake people make is this: they go on a retreat or meet with a life coach (i.e., a professional who walks you through different aspects in your life, where you agree on goals to achieve with their guidance).

They develop meaningful practical maps of their lives, in the form of vision statements (the kind of future you want to have over time), and mission statements or Purpose Statements (which is what you exist for). Then they put them in a cupboard or hide them away in a Bible or book that they hardly read. This is a complete waste if you do that. Therefore, it is important to do everything possible to make your Purpose Statement easy to find and visible.

What you see, you will think more about to gain more clarity. Out of sight, out of mind!

Purpose confusion is a common experience in our society. Such experiences have existed since the beginning of life. No wonder, God was quick to reinforce the purpose of Adam and Eve. Soon after He made them, He said: "Be fruitful, multiply, replenish....subdue the earth..." (Genesis 1: 28).

> ***The Christian sometimes forgets his or her identity in Christ. She forgets that she is sitting in high places with Christ Jesus above principalities and powers. Every little or big challenge shouldn't throw you off a cliff in life. Often, a failed attempt or failure makes***

> ***you feel that it is the end of your life. Likely, it is because you forgot who you're in Christ. Forgetting your identity is a dangerous condition that works against the Christian. You must tap into tools that help you to remember your identity.***

Consequently, Jesus provided a way for us to remember important things through the Holy Spirit:

> *"But the Helper, the Holy Spirit, whom the Father will send in my name, he will teach you all things and bring to your remembrance all that I have said to you"* (John 14:26 ESV).

What foresight? God already knew ahead of time what else you need in addition to your natural self to be whole. Therefore, He provided a supernatural remedy for us. He provided *remembrance through the Holy Spirit* so that He (Holy Spirit) will remind us of all things He has taught us also from the word of God.

Another way that we remember is by keeping the things that we want to remember close to us. We make a bucket list of things we need to buy so that we don't forget to buy the salt, bananas, hot chocolate, and battery for the remote. We make a checklist or a to-do list of things we must do or complete to keep us on track. If you're like me, I place the garbage at the door the night before so that I don't forget to put it out first thing in the morning. All these examples are ways that we make ourselves remember.

> *Forgetting is the reason people lose focus of their purpose. Should you forget to put your energy and time into activities that get you to your purpose, you might nonetheless have been busy for days and weeks. You would have done meaningful, satisfying work and produced some tangible results, but perhaps your efforts didn't contribute to your purpose.*

The challenge is this: people often forget what matters. Because you forgot to focus your energy and time on what is most important to your purpose, most of your work didn't contribute at all or much to your purpose. Should you have remembered what your purpose is, then, you will more likely devote your time and energy to advance it, instead.

This is the reason I insist that creating a visual or picture of your Purpose Statement will help you to stay focused on your purpose. It is no surprise that some teachers encourage you to write down your prayer points to keep your eyes on them while praying. That way you're likely to receive divine insight because you look at them.

Making a list of prayer needs is a similar concept that God taught Habakkuk in the Old Testament. Prophet Habakkuk waited for God to speak to him. God impressed upon his heart to write down the vision He was about to show him:

> *"2And the LORD answered me: "Write the vision; make it plain on tablets, so he may run who reads it. 3For still the vision awaits its appointed time; it hastens to the end—it will not lie. If it seems slow, wait for it; it will surely come; it will not delay"* (Habakkuk 2: 2-3).

The vision, in this case, was information coming from God, supposed to be a blueprint that will guide the people of Israel on how to overcome their enemies. It was the 'how to' of conducting themselves to be free from oppression and threats of their Babylonian enemies.

A vision has some similarities with one's purpose. They both guide the conduct of people's lives. In fact, a Purpose Statement can have elements of a vision since you can have visions (supernatural) that speak about God's plans for you during your purpose discovery process.

Habakkuk's vision has three characteristics:

1. *Written on tablets.*
2. *Made plain.*
3. *People must run with the vision – people must follow the vision.*

Let's look at what each of the three characteristics means.

1. **God instructed Habakkuk to write the vision on tablets:**

Now, what is a tablet? According to Bible history, it is a flat sheet (i.e., pad, plate, or slab) made of wood, stone, clay or bronze or gold upon which information is inscribed. It was onto two pieces of tablets that Moses inscribed the Ten Commandments.

A tablet is an important symbolism in the Bible. It is a vital place to store information. Prophet Habakkuk heard God instructing him to write down the instructions for their deliverance. God ordered him to write the vision specifically on a tablet; a place for which information will be kept safe, not easily stolen or missing. A place where information will be a long-lasting memoire that can hardly be destroyed. Where will you put your purpose statement?

2. **God instructed Habakkuk to make the vision plain.**

To make it plain means not to complicate it. To make the vision plain is write it in *simple plain language* that a grade four student will understand. There must be a reason for God's emphasis on simplicity.

You, too, must not complicate your Purpose Statement. You don't need an advanced dictionary (in any language) to understand your Purpose Statement. Whatever appears complicated needs a second person or others to explain.

If you must explain your written or pictured Purpose Statement before people get what you're up to in life, then it means that it is not simple enough. You have a good understanding of your purpose if you've presented it in such an easy-to-understand manner.

Albert Einstein wrote,

"If you can't explain it to a six-year-old, you don't understand it yourself."

3. **God instructed Prophet Habakkuk to make the vision in such a way that others can read and run with it.**

What does this mean? God is saying to him that he must make the vision accessible to others; others need to be able to see it. When others see the vision, they can run with it. They can follow the vision's instructions, and they can move it from written form to the realm of tangible reality. Remember, the vision was to deliver the Israelites from their enemies; it was a shared vision.

Like Habakkuk's vision, you must create visual imagery or picture of your Purpose Statement that is easy to learn and remember by all viewers and audiences.

Therefore, should you place your Purpose Statement

- On the wall in your office?
- In your bedroom?
- In your living room?
- In your study room?
- In your prayer room?
- On your phone and other gadgets?
- On a T-Shirt, you wear often, etc.?

Yes, yes, yes! Any location that makes your Purpose Statement obvious and crystal clear to others is what will get people's attention.

Although your Purpose Statement is unique to you and not others, making it accessible to others this way allows helpers to join you to achieve your purpose. There are many stories of people whose ideas or discovered purpose was published on YouTube, Facebook, Twitter, Instagram, and other platforms. And because of the reach of social media, they are spotted by investors, designers, producers, and philanthropists, leading to an expanded career, activities, or pursuits within their purpose.

We must learn from Habakkuk's vision. Your purpose statement must be like Habakkuk's vision. Therefore:

Your Purpose Statement must be:

- ✓ ***Written in a safe place such as a journal, computer, or other gadgets.***
- ✓ ***Written in plain language to be easily understood.***
- ✓ ***Available to others so that they can see it and assist you to achieve it.***

Now, let's create a picture representation of a Purpose Statement. This can be a piece of art that summarizes your purpose very broadly. Put your creativity in it!

Sample Purpose Statement from Figure 1

I love to counsel, evangelize, and learn and share new things/skills [Passions & Pains] by researching, teaching/training, analyzing, cooking, and singing [Abilities & Potentials] to **bring peace, hope, salvation, solutions, fulfillment, and health to people's lives [Impact on others],** WHICH CONSEQUENTLY BRING ME JOY, FULFILLMENT, AND PROVISION [IMPACT ON MY LIFE].

I have transformed this Purpose Statement into something photographic, which can be remembered more easily. This is your opportunity to make something unforgettable that you can place on your wall at home or in the office. We will use my sample Purpose Statement to create a visual representation.

Figure 3. Picture Purpose Statement

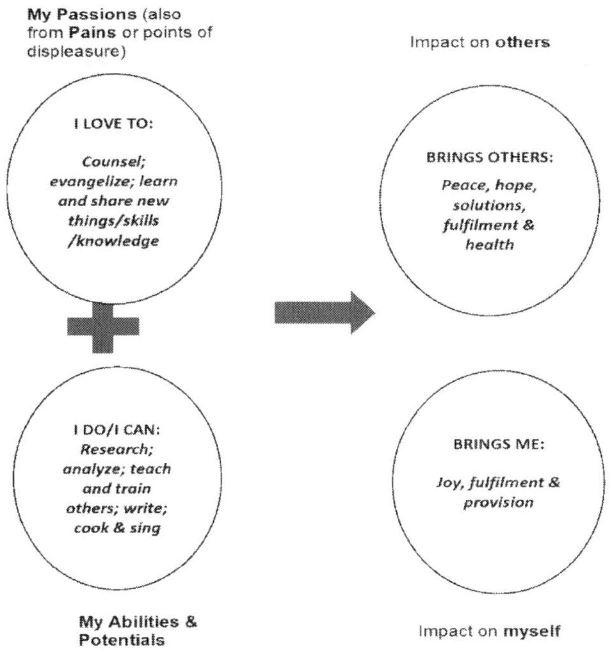

In the next section, I will show you how to choose activities or activity themes that align with your Purpose Statement.

Detailed Picture Purpose: Activities and Activity Themes

With your Purpose Statement, you will identify activity themes and particular activities, including careers that match your APPP information. Include the activities and activity themes in your Picture Purpose Statement in Figure 3, to create your Detailed Picture Purpose (DPP).

So, Figure 3 will help to create the details of your purpose. The passions and pains generally shape the activities to which you apply your abilities and potentials. Using the worksheet information in Table 3 on page 122/123 we draw on the identified passions and pains to tease out activities of interest.

From the information in Table 3, one of the activities that I will love to do is to provide health and wellness coaching, teaching and researching about sicknesses since sickness is one of my pain issues. Look closely at how this example of a specific activity I will enjoy connects with my abilities (teaching, researching). Every activity must be connected to the four rows of Table 3; these are the resources that steer or shape my specific purpose.

Further, there are several career or other possibilities. I could also train as a *medical doctor* in any specialization related to curing the physical body, or as a *psychologist* to heal the mind through *counselling*, or as a *life coach* where I guide others to follow the right career. Also, I could *research and teach* in fields of career development, training development, or generally in *psychology, education and health and wellness.*

Another thing I could do is to train as a teacher of the Bible (i.e., *theologian*) to teach Bible truths through *evangelism*, to the church, in outreach, in marriage and parenting seminars. You can't run out of meaningful, satisfying things to do when you reflect on your purpose.

Discovering your process doesn't end completely while you live. However, you can have a solid Purpose Statement, and DPP for a period. Over time, you can have additional abilities, potentials, passions, and pains (APPP) as you experience new things and situations. The additional APPP is used to revise your Purpose

Statement and DPP. Broadly, your Purpose Statement steers all the activities that you do in life, and the DPP steers the activities to accomplish your purpose. See the DPP in Figure 5, page 146.

Figure 4: Life's Purpose Discovery Cycle (LPDC)

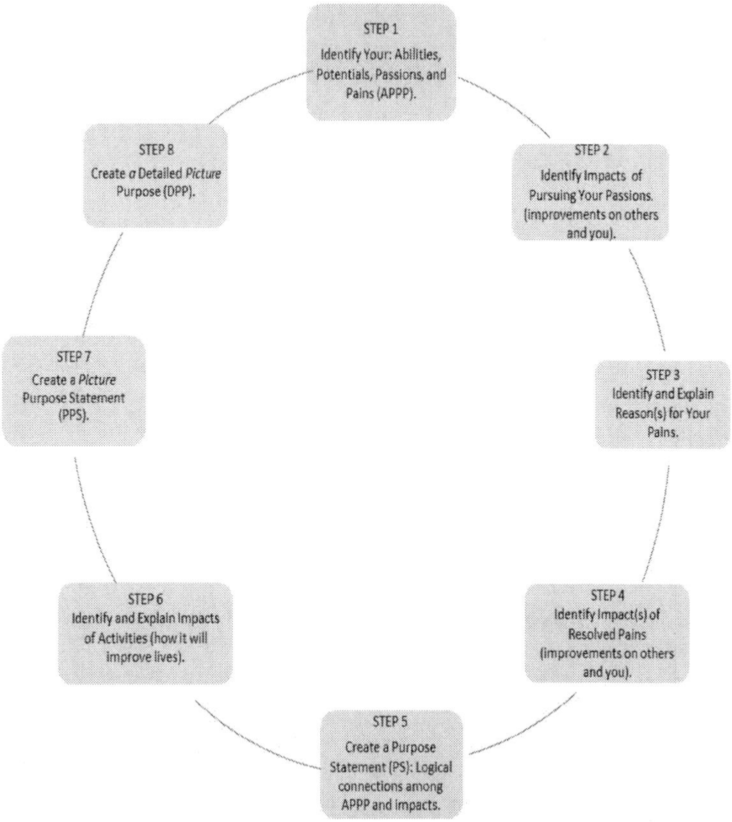

Looking at Figure 4, Life's Purpose Discovery Cycle (LPDC), you see that your Purpose Statement can keep expanding and changing over the course of your life. You may have new passions, abilities, potentials, and pains. The new set of APPP is used to modify your Purpose Statement and DPP.

Now, let's go and populate the Picture Purpose Statement (PPS) with the activities/activity themes that I have listed in Table 3, on page 122/123. This will produce the DPP as we have on the next page.

Figure 5: Detailed Picture Purpose (DPP)

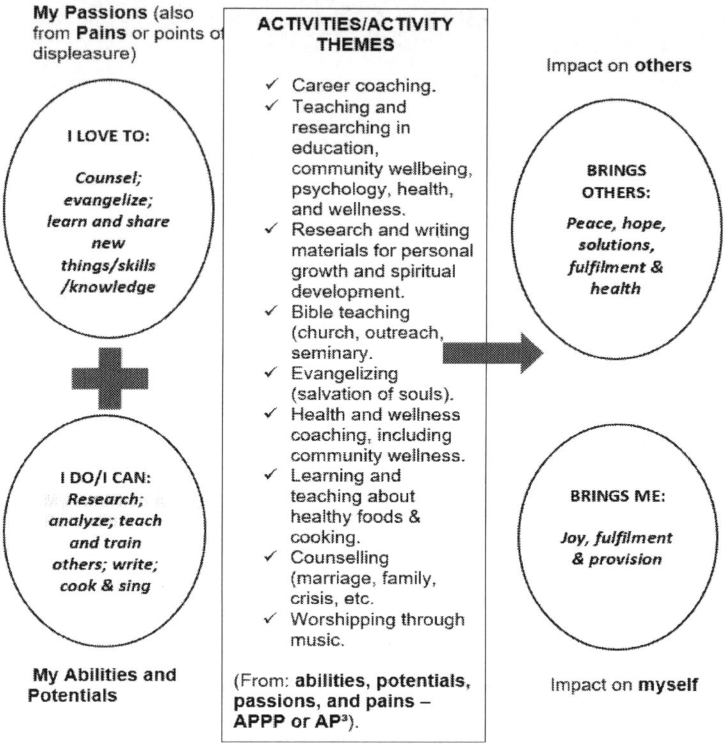

In this chapter, we have seen that the *product* of a Purpose Statement, written in plain language and accessible to you and others, along with activities, programs and projects that align with your Purpose Statement, is the

Detailed Picture Purpose (DPP). By selecting and carrying out activities that align with themes and content in your DPP, you bring your purpose to fruition. With this:

- ***You can't forget your purpose.***
- ***You're ready to make purpose-driven decisions.***
- ***Your helpers know exactly what you're up to and have a glimpse of what could be beneficial to you in making your purpose a reality.***

However, your DPP must not move beyond the paper or gadgets where you recorded it unless you have established strong reasons to carry out activities listed there.' In the next chapter, I will examine principles to guide you when selecting the activities to carry out. I explore why your priority must be to improve lives in all activities you do from your DPP, which I call a 'compelling why.'

Chapter 9

Why Activities within Your Purpose Must Improve Lives

You're on your way to your favourite zoo in Calgary, Alberta (Canada). You're halfway through from Fort McMurray; you've three and half more hours to arrive. Your six and eight-year-old daughters, Amanda and Yan look forward to playing with the dolphins and kangaroos. It is exciting for you. You know your girls will be better off than if you stayed home the whole time during the Easter long weekend. ***What will make you choose to carry out one activity, and not the other, or do nothing?***

Often people focus on the budget, or cost or what appears nice or the trend. When it comes to your purpose, your primary focus must be about changing lives for the better. Your activities must not only match with your discovered purpose but also improve lives, which keeps you motivated. This is your compelling number one reason for any activity. In this chapter, I will highlight the principles to guide you in choosing activities that would inspire motivation and positive change. Also, I will discuss growth processes that inspire you to act on your discovered purpose.

Are Your Reasons 'Legit' or Compelling, But for Who?

What you do must bring positive change in society, and motivate you by making sure it speaks to your discovered purpose (to your passions and pains).

> *On one of my trips to Ghana, I sat next to a brilliant middle-aged man on the flight. I don't miss out on my chit-chat; you never know the connections you could make. Within a few minutes, this new "friend," Jonathan, had already let out his concerns about African governments and what needs to be done. He said it was already his second attempt standing for elections in his constituency in Ghana. I asked him, 'Why are you driven to get into politics?' He said: 'I want to show them how it is done right, there is too much corruption in the system.'*
>
> *I said to myself, hmmm, wait until the going gets tough, when the old boys' club who don't want change,*

> *start fighting your well-meaning efforts to bring positive lasting change. My thoughts continued, 'wanting to show them how to do it right won't stand the test of time; it won't keep you in politics, although this is legitimate (makes sense) reason.' Then, I gathered courage and said to him: my dear friend, you need a much more compelling reason for wanting to get rid of corruption, which had plagued the nation for many decades.*

Jonathan's rationale for becoming a member of parliament was impressive. I admired his passion to serve his country after spending over three decades elsewhere. He will make a superb leader given the exceptional experience he had shared with me. But wait a moment, he doesn't have a 'compelling reason.' His wanting to show them how to do it right isn't good enough. And obviously, wanting to make a good fortune by getting into politics is neither compelling.

The Secret is this:

What is key is the ***positive impact*** on the people who use your product or whom you serve, and how it fulfills your purpose. But what will motivate you?

- ✓ It is the patients that you see feeling better that will keep you in the Emergency Room Physician job.
- ✓ It is the happy faces of moms and dads still together with their children that will keep you in that marriage and family counselling job.
- ✓ For the tradesman or an engineer drilling borehole for communities, what keeps you motivated is seeing that the village children will no longer suffer from hepatitis B because they won't drink from the infected stream. Also, it excites you that because of your boreholes, the children can spend time to studying and playing, and moms can choose to spend more time on the farm or in their businesses because they no longer must walk three kilometres one way to the dirty stream to get water.

The impact of your activities on your own life keeps you driven in the office, field, and on the frontlines even when no one is looking or when the conditions are challenging.

Could Jonathan's reason for going into politics be more compelling? It is better that he is motivated to get the struggling urban street kids off to safe homes and to offer training and self-employment opportunities to reduce poverty. Perhaps Jonathan is hard-wired as a helper, and this is how he feels fulfilled?

- **In whatever you do, you must understand *why* you're doing it to maintain your motivation.**

Losing interest in something you have your heart in is a reality that you can overcome. It is not always because it is outside the boundaries of your purpose, or that it is not improving lives. Human factors such as work overload, having competing demands, and unexpected situations invade your mind, heart, and time; this can throw you off it.

I once took a job that I felt God led me into because of an affirming dream I had several weeks before the opportunity came. About 15 months into it, my heart was pointing in a different direction and worry set it. For a couple of months, I was a wreck. One day, I took the matter to God in prayer. I had some peace. A few days later, I heard American motivational and Christian author and speaker, Joyce Meyer, preaching about 'fatigue.' I was reminded about letting God do it.

Then another day, I got a word in my heart:

> *If you ever get fatigued from doing what I have called you to do, it is likely you're doing it wrongly. In other words, you're doing something the wrong way.*

What does fatigue in your life mean? Perhaps, for you, your fatigue means you need to rest, so rest! God will not discourage you from doing your purpose, but He will show you a more excellent, stress-free, peaceful way to do your purpose (1 Corinthians 12:31).

In my case, I didn't understand certain things about the job, even though it had a tremendous impact. After seeking God about the situation, I understood that the job was for a season and that it was time to take a different direction. I was able to move on, my peace was restored.

We need to keep searching to understand the activities we do. We wouldn't know everything in one day. Peter's life teaches us about allowing God to build that compelling reason for the activities we do.

Peter's Approach: A Compelling Reason at Work

God has his way of leading you to the reasons for the purpose activities that you must focus on. Apostle Paul was one of the disciples whom Jesus worked closely with to establish compelling reasons to fulfill his purpose of preaching the gospel. He had a series of experiences with Jesus before he became a devoted and fiery preacher, whose messages won multitudes to Christ, and who died for the gospel.

Let's see *three* things that make Peter extra-ordinary:

1. Peter was among the first set of disciples that Jesus called: Simon (called Peter) and his brother Andrew together (Matthew 4: 18).
2. Peter was the only disciple who had a revealed understanding of who Jesus was.

3. Peter was with Jesus the whole time in those three-and-half years of ministry on earth before his death.

Jesus Christ let Peter know his purpose from the very day he called him out from fishing to become a fisher of souls for the kingdom.

> *"[18]As Jesus was walking beside the Sea of Galilee, He saw two brothers, Simon called Peter and his brother Andrew. They were casting a net into the sea, for they were fishermen. [19]"Come, follow Me," Jesus said, "and I will make you fishers of men." [20]And at once they left their nets and followed Him" (*Matthew 4: 18-20*).*

Take note that Jesus said, he is the one who will ***make*** Peter a fisher of men (preacher of the good news). Have you thought that you will ***make yourself*** learn how to do your purpose or will God's spirit navigate this purpose in you as you submit your will?

Peter understood deep spiritual things from time to time. For example, he was the only disciple who answered correctly when Jesus asked: "But who do you say that I am?" Peter answered and said, "You are the Christ, the Son of the living God" (Matthew 15:16). Jesus was amazed because Peter received this information from God's Spirit – Peter had a revelation!

However, because of fear of getting tortured like Jesus, Peter denied knowing Jesus three times when He (Jesus) was arrested. But Jesus didn't give up on Peter. Earlier, Jesus had called Peter the rock on which God will build the church (Matthew 16:18). When Jesus resurrected, revealing himself to Peter and others, and showing them his nail-wounded-scars, now, they can believe Jesus' words even more. Those instances validated Jesus' promise:

> *"He told them, "This is what is written: The Messiah will suffer and rise from the dead on the third day"* (Luke 24:46).

Jesus was committed to ensuring that Peter had several compelling reasons to follow his purpose of preaching the gospel. When Jesus resurrected, he placed Peter in a position of honour by commissioning him to God's work even after Peter had denied Him three times. Jesus said to him: "feed my lamb," "take care of my sheep" and "feed my sheep," if you indeed love me. These experiences *inspired* Peter to return to preaching, given that there was no doubt that Jesus was (and is) truly the Son of God, and that Peter must do the assignment.

However, Peter must wait to receive the Holy Spirit before preaching. Jesus had told the disciples to stay in Jerusalem (Acts 1:8) until they've received power from the Holy Spirit. This was supposed to happen after Jesus returns to His Father in heaven following His resurrection.

> "[1] *When the day of Pentecost came, they were all together in one place.* [2] *Suddenly a sound like the blowing of a violent wind came from heaven and filled the whole house where they were sitting.* [3] *They saw what seemed to be tongues of fire that separated and came to rest on each of them.* [4] *All of them were filled with the Holy Spirit and began to speak in other tongues as the Spirit enabled them"* (Acts 2: 1-4).

As Jesus promised, the Holy Spirit, the one who empowers and teaches, came upon Peter with the other 120 disciples and followers in the upper room on the day of Pentecost (i.e., 50 days after his resurrection). They had enough evidence to believe every word that Jesus had told them before and after he resurrected. Peter was persuaded and motivated by the proof of Jesus's divinity and power, wanting to improve lives, and by the upper room outpouring of the Holy Spirit.

So, perhaps he said to himself, 'my assignment to win souls and establish the preaching of the gospel must be accomplished.

Peter begun. That very day, he astonished the crowd with so much authority. It was recorded that:

> *"[37]When the people heard this [Peter's preach], they were cut to the heart and said to Peter and the other apostles, "Brothers, what shall we do?" [38]Peter replied, "Repent and be baptized, every one of you, in the name of Jesus Christ for the forgiveness of your sins. And you will receive the gift of the Holy Spirit. [39]The promise is for you and your children and for all who are far off—for all whom the Lord our God will call"* (Acts 2: 37-39).

His message triggered conviction and surrender as it 'cut to the heart,' therefore, the crowd who heard Peter's message responded, they repented and received Christ. This was also why on the same day, 3,000 souls gave their lives to Christ, adding to the 120.

As you can see, three things that moved Peter to keep on the path of preaching were undeniable:

1. The integrity of Jesus' words.
2. His encounter with the resurrected Jesus.
3. The equipping by the Holy Spirit.

Peter responded to these experiences with obedience. His purpose was to be a fisher of men. So, he followed that path.

WHAT ABOUT YOU?

- ***Is your experience with the word of God proven that every promise in His word and your purpose (the good plans for you) will be established (i.e., integrity: promise matches actual experience)?***

- ***Are you aware that your passions, desires, and abilities are what God wants you to follow to bring value to others,' and do well on earth?***
- ***Do you desire supernatural experiences to confirm your purpose and give you compelling reasons why you must pursue them? Then, ask God.***
- ***Have you received the baptism of the Holy Spirit? God must equip you by this Holy Spirit to step out into your purpose and be victorious.***

You may have started carrying out an activity (or something) without the full understanding and have fallen out. God wants to give you compelling reasons to get back into your purpose with full force as Peter did. Don't give up. Living your purpose is worth it; your purpose benefits others and benefits you.

What's in it for Peter and others?

Both Peter and the people got their share of benefit as Peter preached the gospel. Peter could not be selfish and say, 'It is my life; I will do whatever I want to do and whenever I want to do it.' People's salvation – entering eternal life depended on him. He needed to act fast, and not be indecisive. Preaching the gospel will positively impact Peter (i.e., give him joy knowing that he is obeying his master and that he will be cared for through his preaching (1 Timothy 5:18).

Not only will Peter receive a reward in heaven, preaching the gospel brings others a better life on earth and heaven. He didn't quit no matter the challenges. He followed the path of his purpose until he died a martyr. He could die for the gospel because of the empowerment of the Holy Spirit. He was compelled by his purpose to have lives snatched from the enemy (fish for souls) and obedience to Christ who He believes in.

> *I think of my life and what gets me up in the morning. My passion is to see that Christians and everyone are inspired to start taking steps to follow their purpose. I desire to see them have a blessed life that gives glory to God and draws others to believe in Christ. So, I was compelled and kept writing this book even when it didn't feel like a good day to write. I kept my mind*

focused on my conviction that people's lives will improve by reading this book.

You must keep your heart on your 'compelling why.' Focus on the change your purpose will bring to people's lives and yours; this is what compels you to keep going even through those challenging times.

In concluding this chapter, I emphasize you must examine your activities carefully to ensure that improvement is a primary reason you do it. It is not alright to just do things; you must have sound reasons that bring positive change. You won't know everything in one day; you will be taught by God (through the Holy Spirit) as you yield to Him every step in the purpose journey.

A discovered purpose that you don't use obstructs all the exciting possibilities you can have. In the following chapter, we will look at how to use your discovered purpose to make important decisions that align with your life's purpose.

Chapter 10

Your Purpose and Important Decisions

Making decisions about any aspect of your life is an important task that you must take seriously. You have made many decisions and so have others. People have attended the wrong or right school, dated the wrong or right person, accepted the wrong job, refused the right job and married the wrong or right spouse by the decisions they made. All these decisions have consequences; they might lead to blessings (i.e., things going the way you imagined and even better eventually because the choices you made aligned with God's will).

Or it could lead to curses (i.e., difficulties that you allowed into your life because of wrong choices). When you look among your friends, acquaintances, or family, you can find people you know who have made one wrong choice or another, who suffered or are suffering as a result. In the same way, you would find those who made good choices who are enjoying those choices. A right decision will lead to blessings, peace, joy, and fulfillment.

In this chapter, I will illustrate how to use Detailed Picture Purpose (DPP) (with the Abilities, Potentials, Passions and Pains [APPP] and Purpose Statement) to make career decisions that will advance your purpose while paying attention to influencers that can lead you to the wrong or right way. I guide you with tools and strategies that will help you to ensure alignment between your detailed picture purpose and decisions around your career, which is key to entering and remaining in your purpose.

Matching Life's Choices with Your Purpose

We are making decisions in a world where people are often quick to give us advice. I call them "influencers." We receive advice even in areas where they haven't obtained life-changing experiences or are yet to master. Everyone, young or old, has a useful life experience. It appears that information and help abound, discovering and living one's purpose is an unclear area. It is never too late to turn things around and live your purpose wherever you're in your life.

❖ **"Anyone who has never made a mistake has never tried anything new"** (Albert Einstein).

Once you have discovered your life's purpose, you have taken care of a big chunk of your key tasks in life. You're on your way to amaze your world.

An architect who intends to build a spectacular house must first have a blueprint - a drawing of the house. It is interesting that I am referring to a house as if it is your life! Yes, yes, yes, your life is your house, your house is your life. When I dream and it is about a house, it has something to do with my life. So, walk with me through this house or life we are building.

Why should you have a blueprint? Building a mud house or a couple of rooms on a piece of remote or rural land might not entail an elaborate drawing or a blueprint.

❖ *If you know how sophisticated God made you and the sophisticated gifts and talents He placed in you, you will do the smart thing; you will work with God to discover the blueprint of your elaborate life*.

Having a blueprint (i.e., your discovered purpose) means you have made some choices already. It means that you have an idea about the right size of the various compartments or areas of the house. You have envisioned the right materials and the right colours for the house that you're constructing. You know what kind of roof you will put on the house so that you will approach the right supplier. Having a blueprint means you have the details of what must go into building the house. It is less stressful when this clear blueprint embedded with choices is guiding the construction of your house.

Life is full of choices and so you must choose. In this generation of abundant advancements in science and technology, we have many opportunities. It gets overwhelming having so many options from which we must choose. At a restaurant, there can be so many options on the menu. Take chicken alone, and there will be gazillion varieties of how they have been prepared: salt and pepper fried; grilled in honey and garlic; coated with crumbs, seasoned, and fried; and steamed in spices and tomato sauce. You must choose. You get a particular flavour and taste depending on what you choose.

Such is our life. Each choice leads to an outcome. Each choice has a specific taste to it that will be felt in your mouth and stomach. If it has pepper seasoning, it is likely going to burn in your mouth and stomach. If it is mild, it means you will notice little to no spice in your mouth and stomach. Your choice must align with your blueprint to produce the outcome that you desire.

Choosing to Match Purpose: Reducing Risks

Choice-making is an inevitable part of life, it is both an opportunity and a challenge. Every choice comes with a certain level of risk. Nigerian tele-evangelist of blessed memory, Dr. Benson Idahosa, once said, "It is riskier not to take a risk." You must choose even if it means it is risky.

- How are you making choices?
- Are you one of those people who gamble to arrive at a choice – you throw the dice in the air and hope that it lands on six so that you could have spicy chicken or steak?

- Do you, out of lust, follow the sexually attractive looks of a man or woman and blindly fall in love, only to fall out of love in no time?
- Do you say yes to that job because you need just anything to do, or because the money and benefits look good?

Because you're a passionate, praying, Holy Spirit-filled Christian, doesn't mean that whatever comes to your doorstep is an opportunity you should grab.

Let's Find Out Why?

Like God, Satan also answers prayers. How? A lady, Satanist, who operated in witchcraft, revealed a mystery about prayer. After becoming free, she spoke about how witches work against reckless Christians. She said, their prayers arrive in the demonic realm when they don't ask God to forgive their sins. She explained that, ideally, the prayer of the believer goes up from the earth through the first heaven (sky), past the second layer of heaven (i.e., where Satan and demonic forces are) and arrives at the final third heaven (i.e., where God receives prayers). But for the sinner, the prayer goes through the first heaven and then gets trapped in the second heaven, and those prayers don't get to God. She added that, sometimes, they respond to the sinner's prayers.

Supposing, the person asked for work, a spouse, you name it. They package an answer and send it to the sinner. They can send you a job, car, boyfriend, house, or spouse. And in no time, you begin to experience chaos and calamity. You get trapped into more sin and more destruction. You become a prey of the enemy, if you embrace whatsoever comes your way, without seeking God to know if it is His will.

Also, the decisions you make must align with your purpose. What kinds of opportunities are coming to you? Are you going to disregard what appears good, but does not fit into your purpose? People have been stretched so thin because they take on everything that comes their way. By so doing, they are unable to invest more time and effort into those things that are within their purpose. Again:

> *"A kingdom that is divided against itself cannot stand"* (Mark 3:24).

- ***Being divided and spreading yourself thin will not allow you to invest adequate energy, time, and money on what will matter to your purpose.***

- ***Constantly align your decisions with what you have discovered is your purpose.***

- ***Measure whether you've made a good decision by the extent to which the decision contributes to and/or advances your purpose.***

I love this saying: *"If you don't know where you are going, any road will take you there."* The truth is that life is not always in a fine perfectly structured order where you will know all things and know ahead of time how you will respond to all situations. However, when you have Picture Purpose Statement along with selected activities or activity themes (i.e., DPP), you can respond quickly and meaningfully to opportunities and challenges. This is because you already have a blueprint (or road map) for your purpose – which guides you even during the most spontaneous decision moments you will face.

Suppose you find out at your workplace or school about an exchange program to learn first-class wedding designs with an opportunity to be in a fashion show at a world top design college – would you go or not go? You will know quickly whether this could be for you if you already have a detailed picture of your Purpose Statement (which includes your selected activities – DPP). You will consider this opportunity if learning about more sophisticated wedding designs and connections with accomplished wedding clothes designers in the industry would assist your career, looking at your discovered purpose. You won't be confused, neither would you delay or miss this opportunity.

People who make spontaneous decisions against their purpose find out down the road that, although they have been busy doing some things, they didn't achieve progress on their purpose.

- Life's events and opportunities don't always warn you before they happen. That's why you must be always ready with your detailed picture purpose.

- Avoid mistakes by always having your detailed picture purpose close to you to refer to in the event you must make a spontaneous decision.

Proverbs 11:14 says:

> *"Where there is no guidance the people fall, but in an abundance of counsellors there is victory."*

Your guide includes your Detailed Picture Purpose (DPP), Purpose Statement (PS) and Abilities, Potentials, Passions and Pains (APPP), along with the well-meaning and knowledgeable people who can counsel you. And we have seen how to make career decisions after you have discovered your purpose. Consequently, your DPP becomes your map for selecting careers that align with your purpose, and some guidance from others can be helpful. However, be careful not to be misguided by these 'influencers.'

The Influencers of Career Decisions

It is common to follow the crowd to pursue what others are going after, to follow trends – what appears to be making money, sense, or fancy. Growing up in a time and place in Ghana where career counselling was not formally available at school, I got career advice mostly from family, peers, and acquaintances. My teachers took interest in sharing their thoughts on school choice and programs, especially for postsecondary education. The teachers who shared their knowledge and experiences with me were not necessarily trained career guidance counsellors, although some were well-experienced and guided well. Career decision-making continues to be a puzzling subject everywhere around the world.

Often, we like to mimic others. It appears easier to follow what others are doing because you don't have to chart your own path. In fact, observing others in their careers can generate interest in you as an observer. Research in the discipline of career education mentions the effect of what is known as '*Cultural capital.*' ***Cultural capital*** (originated in the 1970s by French Sociologist Pierre Bourdieu), *is a collection of symbolic elements (social assets) such as skills, tastes, clothing, habits, certificates (credentials), and material things you own (material belongings)* *that help you to progress in society. Cultural capital here originates from the family and is passed on to other members of the family (Bourdieu, 1986).*

Therefore, it is common to find that certain families are known for specific careers or fields. You may find most people in a family lean towards the trades such as welding, construction, automobile mechanics, bakery and restaurant or hospitality type of work. In another family, most of them could be into health careers, working as doctors, nurses, physiotherapists, naturopaths, and dentists. There is a kind of familiarity with the health or trades fields that occurs by observing, participating and just being a family member. ***You pick up certain interests, aspirations, dispositions, and tastes from the family. Therefore, your family can influence your choice of career and other decisions.***

Other kinds of capital exist. One of them is *social capital,* which you acquire by associating with a group.

> *Social capital comes from "networks together with shared norms, values and understandings that facilitate co-operation within or among groups"* (Organization

for Economic Corporation and Development's [OECD], 2014).

By knowing someone and having certain things in common with that person, you can connect and support each other. Your connection with the group creates certain biases or interests and they affect your choices.

I find that people follow certain career paths because of the community or groups to which they belong. If you attend a church where several young men and young women are into shipping and receiving goods (i.e., clearing and forwarding), you will realize that your conversations are about clearing/receiving/shipping/forwarding. Either you're influencing others, or they are influencing you into this career.

This is because certain ambitions, tastes, norms, and values are passed on to one another because of the shared relationship. This is how, over time, you notice that most of your friends including you are into similar fields of work that are common among your social networks. All such influences guide the decisions about your career.

Is it Wrong If You Are Influenced into a Career?

Our families and our social networks in particular influence us in various ways. Supposing you don't know your purpose, and you follow family interests and preferences, it can result in a fulfilling life, if that is what God has hard-wired you to do; meaning your abilities, potential, passions and pains (APPP) match that career.

There is the possibility that some families carry similar APPPs.

> ***My friend, Sarah,*** *has a passion for singing and writing songs. She is a composer and a producer. Her children are also into music. One of her sons is a music composer, producer, and performer. Sarah's uncle played the guitar and sang in and around the village and cities. He spent most of the monetary gifts from his spectators on alcohol. Even when he was drunk, his passion kept him performing. Also, Sarah's grandfather played the accordion. As an old man in his 80s, grandpa played for the kids at home and at gatherings in the village. Some families have similar interests whereas others don't.*

It is common to see a person pursuing several passions. Sometimes, after many years of a career in medicine, a doctor will turn to develop his or her passions in music, motivational speaking, engineering, or counselling. Therefore, you can wear more than one hat by following your various passions.

The APPP that God has placed inside you can't be silenced. They scream for expression if you don't attend to them. It is extremely uncomfortable and unsettling for a devoted Christian appearing to have money, a nice life and a family that is well taken care of, still discovering that a passion remains unattended to – and feeling lost.

- ***If you're devotedly living for God and serving Him, and feel out of place, this is a good sign that you must take a careful look at what else is in you (i.e., in your APPP) that is begging for expression.***

We know that not having a relationship with God creates an imbalance that can be uncomfortable. It is not surprising that some do harmful things out of this discomfort, which are completely avoidable.

This is perhaps when they realize that there is no real new challenge to conquer. This is where they have completed the challenge of climbing Mountain Everest; produced music that sold the most copies in the world's history or made a scientific discovery recorded in the Guinness Book of Records. For another, it could be you married the woman of your dreams; you have raised children whose successful lives make you an accomplished parent in your eyes and those of your social network. You then ask, 'what next,' and realize, there isn't a new adventure to pursue.

When we think and feel that we have arrived and that there is nothing more to challenge us, fight for or win, this can be risky.

God has made a way out for us, so we don't get stuck in such situations. The remedy is to return to or have a love relationship with the Holy Spirit through Jesus Christ. This love relationship teaches and guides you to many unending possibilities for your life. Living by faith in

Christ and the word of God secures your life. In Christ, you have an unending next big dream to keep you inspired even after several gigantic feats while you're still here.

In this chapter, we have seen that family and social networks can steer the careers we choose. Although not all career choices made this way lead to unfulfilling outcomes. However, being influenced this way to follow choices that are outside God's perspective of your purpose likely won't guarantee healthy, lasting motivation in life. Next, I will guide you through how to apply the knowledge about your discovered purpose to select a corresponding or matching purpose-driven career.

Chapter 11

Making Purpose-Driven Career Decisions

There are several tools for your career planning. These tools help you to identify your fitting careers, although they don't walk you through a step-by-step process to identify your abilities, potentials, passions, and pains (i.e., the key building blocks or backbone of your purpose). This is what makes this book a more practical tool for planning and building your purpose-led life. In this chapter, I will show you how to make decisions using the information of your purpose in the Detailed Picture Purpose (see in Figure 5, page 146).

Choosing a Career that Matches Your Purpose

Let's look at how to pick a career(s) from the activities or activity themes (that I could carry out) listed in my Detailed Picture Purpose (DPP). Choose the career(s) first before the education and training that will prepare you for the chosen career.

In my list of activities or activity themes, let's take *health and wellness coaching*, for example.

Now, ask yourself: what are the possible careers available within this theme?

- Research this activity or activity theme online and in books.
- Speak to a career counsellor/advisor/coach for career ideas within the chosen theme.
- Use this book as a guide.

For example, suppose I choose to be *a counsellor or a health educator* within the ***health and wellness coaching field***, I must find out the kind of education that is required for these jobs.

From my research, I discovered that to be a counsellor or a health educator, I will require academic qualifications in nursing, nutrition, medicine or occupational therapy, social work, or psychology (that is for counselling/mental health work). Also, it requires experience with the client group, practicums, or internships.

It is important that you understand the career and your roles before committing yourself. Let's see examples of careers in health and community health, followed by careers in engineering and their roles.

Examples of Careers in Health and Community Wellness

Most of the examples listed in Table 4 require a university degree or college certification, practicums, and experience.

Table 4: Careers in Health and Community Wellness (not limited to this list)

Career name	Role
Health educator	Designs and implements disease prevention and health promotion programs.
Nutritionist/dietitian	Assess, counsels, and educates patients to ensure a healthy diet and lifestyle.
Fitness director	Oversees the staff and clients' experiences of fitness facilities who encourages healthy active and social lives.
Physical education teacher	Creates and implements curriculum of interest and abilities to students, and sometimes teaches generally about health.
Physical therapist	Delivers and supervises treatments to plan the discharge of patients.
Nurse	Ranges from taking care of critically ill patients to vaccinations. Assess (do exam), educate, counsel,

	and promote, administer medication and other interventions, and co-ordinate care with all health professionals.
Occupational therapist	Helps people to create and maintain satisfying and successful roles and activities to minimize disability and social marginalization in their daily lives. Assesses how people occupy their time and space to discover any issues and interventions.
Crisis counsellor	Provides support and guidance to an individual or a group (family or community) during a situation or event that is overwhelming and difficult coping with, by using community and health system. Goal is to decrease emotional pain and provide emotional support and coping plan and skills.
Psychologist	Assesses mental and behavioural conditions, and diagnoses and communicates any disorders/dysfunctions. Helps individuals to maintain health through consultation, assessment, diagnosis, counselling, and therapy.

Psychiatrist	Identifies and treats medical disorders that interfere with thought processes. Has training in both medical and psychological aspects of behaviour. Has additional unique skills as behavioural psychiatrist and physician.
Psychosocial rehabilitation worker	Provides medical and psychosocial treatment in ways that encourage social interaction, independent living, and vocational performance to restore the function of a person with mental illness in the community
Career coach	Helps to assess interests, abilities, issues, values and goals, and development goals. Supports individuals in finding and maintaining a career and achieving their career goals.
Social work	Assists people to tap into community resources, and own resources to resolve problems and enhance their well-being. Several roles: case manager; court support worker; crisis counsellor; mental health educator; and policy development and training. Serves as a member of a multi-disciplinary team.

Professor/researcher/trainer/instructor	Teaches, researches, and trains others in education, health, spiritual development, and aspects that enhance individual, family, and community life

Source: Government of Ontario (2018).

As you can see, there are a variety of health and wellness kinds of careers. Since you have your DPP with activities or activity themes that will guide choosing your career, you're not overwhelmed. In my case, you can see that I have selected related careers that fit the activities or activity themes that I listed align with my purpose.

In the next diagram, Figure 6, we will look at some careers that best align with my activities or activity themes, which I derived from my APPP.

Figure 6: Health and community wellness matching careers.

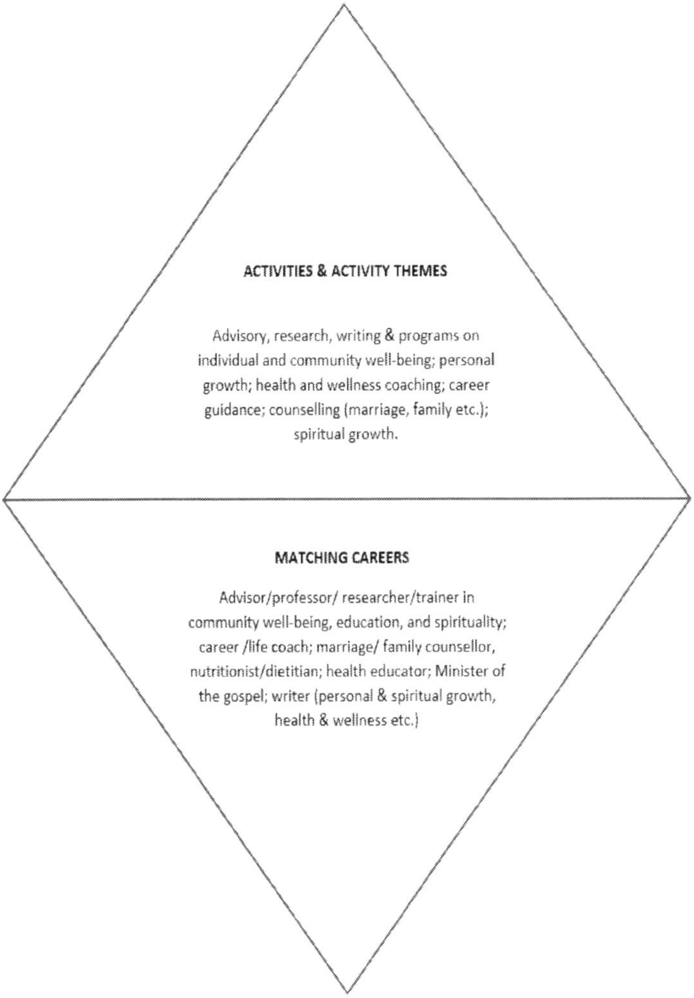

Lets explore careers in engineering.

Examples of Careers in Engineering

What is the reason you will choose to pursue a career in engineering? What are some of the careers in this field and what are the roles?

Engineering is the path for you if you listed a passion to:

- ✓ Build physical systems.
- ✓ Create machinery.
- ✓ Harness natural resources.
- ✓ Generate solutions to environmental problem such as reclaiming waste from resource extraction (oil, gas, and minerals).

There are several specialties in engineering. Information from your research (or with help of a career counsellor) will help you to choose which field of engineering aligns with the activities or activity themes you like, and which education or training program best suits it.

If you choose *software engineering*, for example, you will have several *programs options*. You can take a college-level certificate and diploma. Also, you can choose undergraduate degree options such as applied science, information systems, computer science, electrical engineering, mathematics, and information technology.

Table 5: Careers in Engineering (not limited to this list)

Career name	Role
Aerospace engineer	Designs development and production of aircraft and space craft.
Agricultural engineer	Focuses on land, water, forestry, biofuels, machinery, planning animal environments, and methods of food processing. Also called a biological engineer.
Automotive engineer	Researches, designs, and develops vehicles and their subsystems
Biomedical engineer	Researches, analyses and designs solutions for improving patients' care such as *artificial* organs and body parts (prosthesis). Combines biology, medicine, and engineering.

Chemical engineer	Manipulates atoms and molecules at extremely small size from laboratory to large-scale industrial processes to convert chemicals, raw materials, living cells, micro-organisms and energy into useful products and forms that solves human problems.
Civil engineer	Designs and constructs roads, bridges, buildings, and water systems making sure built structures are compliant with environmental standards and can withstand natural earthquakes and hurricanes.
Computer engineer	Develops and improves software and hardware for computers.
Drafting and design engineer	Designs processes (including material and manufacturing) from start to finish plans.
Electrical engineer	Designs, develops, tests, and supervises power supply, power generation, lighting installations and wiring in aircraft, automobiles, and buildings.

Environmental engineer	Protects and improves environment quality (air, water, and soil) using science and engineering principles. Focus on wastewater management, water-borne diseases, and air pollution management.
Geological engineer	Applies earth science to solve problems by involving geology, civil engineering, forestry, mining, and geography. Studies rock and soil balance; groundwater; environmental issues; construction sites planning; and exploration of fossil fuels and mineral deposits.
Marine engineer	Designs and constructs internal structures (electrical, thrust, and environmental systems) of seagoing ships for oil mining and cruises.
Mechanical engineer	Controls motion, energy and force using human, economic and material mediums to meet society's needs.
Petroleum engineer	Explores, designs, and develops new technology and approaches for extracting oil and gas from wells.

Software engineer	Tests, designs, develops and maintains computer software (programming and applications) for personal and business uses.

Source: EducatingEngineers.com (2017).

With these different fields in *engineering alone*, it can be overwhelming when you must choose at least one field to study at a time. Some may want to pursue several careers if they can't choose one or a few.

Can I Pursue More Than One Career?

By now you have an idea of possible careers you can pursue but narrowing it down to one can be challenging for some.

1. ***Instead of being a jack-of-all trades, you set yourself up for greater success if you specialize in one or two areas.***
2. ***Don't spread yourself thin in trying to pursue many careers.***

Sometimes, you can use one field of training or education to work in more fields. It is important to look for opportunities to maximize one career. In my case, because I studied broadly, social science, specializing in community development and education, it allows me to apply my skills to careers that fit with my selected activity themes. Other specialties may require that I do additional training to become qualified to practice - e.g., to be a dietitian or counsellor.

Therefore, while planning your training and education, consider choosing to train for one career at a time. And if you're making these career decisions later in life after you've had some other training and education, consider an option or level that makes life a bit easier for you, especially if you must (to a large extent) retrain and you have other commitments. Whatever additional skills you gain make you better.

- No skills you have acquired through previous training, work or in life are a waste.
- Your combination of skills produces your uniqueness in what you do.

For example, suppose you studied sound engineering, and you decide to become a counsellor instead, you're likely to use music and sounds in your counselling practice to help clients. You become a unique counsellor specializing in applying sound theories and techniques. You could invent new counselling practice techniques that use sound because of your previous education or training. Therefore, get excited about what will come out of your skill sets when you add another education or training from a closely related or different field.

It is prudent to choose one or two careers as your primary source of livelihood. This way, you can put considerable effort and time into a few things you do well to maximize the benefits. The other roles could be secondary (such as volunteer, part-time and leisure roles). Here, the goal of having these secondary roles is to bring value to others and be fulfilled.

In this chapter, I explained how to decide on careers that correspond with your activity preferences listed in your Detailed Picture Purpose. This way you will choose careers that match your purpose to ensure that your work is fulfilling and provides for you. In the next chapter, we will explore further how to choose your education and training and other tools to understand yourself in the process.

Chapter 12

Planning Your Education and Tools for Understanding Yourself

Having relevant information that helps to uncover more systematically your purpose comes with a responsibility to complete the corresponding education and training. Aside from the following tools; ***1. Abilities, Potentials, Passions, and Pains (APPP), 2. Purpose Statement and 3. Detailed Picture Purpose (DPP)***, you may wonder if other popular tools can help with discovering your purpose. There is a myriad of psychology-based personality testing tools that can deepen understanding of yourself, although they don't adequately prepare you to discover God's intended purpose for humanity (i.e., grand purpose) and your specific purpose flowing from it.

In this chapter, I discuss the next steps in planning your education. Also, I explore the role of personality assessment tools along with tools created for you in this book to support your decisions.

Planning Your Education: Things to Think About

It is important to consider situations that can impact your educational success. Getting ahead of yourself by thinking through your personal circumstances as well as what is required from the institution and the conditions for success will better position you for success.

The following are <u>things you must consider</u> while planning for your education/training or retraining:

a. What did I find from researching into my possible careers?

b. What training is required to work in my chosen career?

c. Does it matter to me which specific specialty within the broad career field that I pursue? For example, do I want to be a general nurse or pediatric nurse?

d. Do I have the pre-requisites for the program I have chosen?

e. Do I already have some of the education and skills for getting into this field? Do I already have some of the course credits that can be transferred into my chosen program?

f. What education/training delivery options are available - online versus in-person or a combination? Which option(s) works with my current lifestyle and commitments (e.g., spouse, children, and family)?

g. How much will my education/training cost?

h. Will money to finance my education/training be available? Do I need more savings or other sources? Do I qualify for a loan if I need it? Are scholarships available to which I can apply?

i. How long does it take to train in this field?

j. Should I be concerned about whether jobs will be available right after completion? Is there a wait time before I can start my first job? If so, generally, how long is the wait?

k. When can I start school or training?

l. When will I finish the school or training given a potential start date?

m. Are practicums, volunteer hours or internship placements a required part of the training? Will these help me to obtain a job?

These questions are a part of your education and training planning so that you can proactively handle any barriers and make use of opportunities. All these questions need you to make clear choices. It is evident that an individual's personality determines the choices that suit him or her.

In the next section, I will present tools that help you to understand your personality and how that shapes your decisions.

Tools for Understanding Your Personality

Your personality is your uniqueness. Your personality is a characteristic pattern of thoughts, feelings and behaviour that is distinct or unique to you. This set of characteristics in behaviour, mind and emotions comes from biological composition and environment. Our personalities are accompanied by certain abilities, potentials, passions, and pains. ***Your personality influences the kind of tendencies and choices to which you're drawn.*** From many years of studies, psychologists have developed patterns of behaviour, thinking and feelings seen within various groups, forming distinct types of personality groups and their unique characteristics (Matthews, 2019).

There are several tools built from the understanding of personalities that help you to understand your tendencies – such as the kinds of careers you may like. These are called *personality assessments*.

Personality assessments are pointers to your uniqueness. Such tools can guide you to discover and validate your greatest potentials that you can harness for success. Generally, personality assessments tell your preferences around the following:

> ***your intrinsic/core values; sources of motivation; sources of stress; style of communication; self-esteem; language patterns; non-verbal reactions; social skills; listening styles; mental states; orientation to relationship; and ethical behaviours*** (Matthews, 2019).

Let's look briefly at some of the personality assessment tools.

Personality Assessment Tools

i. **True colours**: use four central colours (Orange, Gold, Green, and Blue) to reveal your different motivations, actions, and communication styles. The idea is that everyone is made of a combination of all four colours (comprising a range) but one is often most dominant (True Colours, 2021).

ii. **Myers-Briggs type indicator:** Assesses several factors on a scale and groups people according to the following factors: information gathering, world focus, decision-making approach, and interaction approach. The extreme opposites of these factors are introversion versus extroversion; thinking versus feeling; sensing versus intuition, and; judging versus perceiving. How the strongest traits interrelate is the basis for grouping people. This is most widely used in business (Matthews, 2019, Psychology Today, 2021).

iii. **CliftonStrengths**: Assesses the presence of talent in 34 areas with the help of 177 questions. The report from this assessment provides personalized insights that can help an individual to understand what he or she naturally does best (Matthews, 2019, Psychology Today, 2021).

iv. **16 Personality factor (pf) questionnaire:** Assesses 16 personality dimensions, including social boldness, warmth, openness to change, self-reliance, and perfectionism. These produce a general understanding of the individual that can predict behaviours. The assessment organizes an individual by independence, extraversion, self-control, anxiety, and tough-mindedness (Matthews, 2019, Psychology Today, 2021).

v. **California Psychological Inventory (CPI)**: Offers information on work-related characteristics such as understanding of concepts, independence, and sociability (social skills). This is important for determining how employees will interact with others and react under specific situations (Matthews, 2019, Psychology Today, 2021).

vi. **Caliper Profile**: Assesses more than 25 personality traits important for job performance. It takes stock of one's strengths, weaknesses, and potentials, which helps to understand motivators as well as empathy, leadership, and time management. What may be a weakness (e.g., aggressiveness) in one job role might be a strength in another job role (Matthews, 2019, Psychology Today, 2021).

vii. **Gallup StrengthsFinder**: This personality assessment tool assesses the strengths of the individual by guiding you to select five top strengths out of a total of 34 possible strengths characteristics around helpfulness, positivity, and achievement. Since the intention is to expand traits that support workplace success, it ignores any potential negatives (Matthews, 2019, Psychology Today, 2021).

viii. **Five factor model:** is a model that divides into five traits: 1. Conscientiousness, 2. Agreeableness, 3. Openness to Experience, 4. Neuroticism, and 5. Extroversion (CANOE or OCEAN). They are measured on scales. An individual may be highly extraverted. An individual low in extraversion is introverted or is somewhere in-between the two extremes (De Janasz, Dowd & Schneider, 2021).

Explore the following personality tests online to see where you're placed. You may find them revealing and interesting.

Free Personality Tests

1. Wall Street Academy (2021). My personality test. https://my-personality-test.com/
2. NERIS Analytics Limited (2021). 16 Personalities. Free Personality Test. https://www.16personalities.com/free-personality-test
3. Free psychological tests (2021). https://www.123test.com/disc-personality-test/
4. Testcolor (2021). Your free personality test. http://www.testcolor.com/personalitytest/personalitytest.php
5. Potter, J. (2016). The big five project personality test. https://www.outofservice.com/bigfive/
6. Teambuilding (2021). 24 Free personality tests for team building in 2021. https://teambuilding.com/blog/personality-tests

Use these personality tests to learn more about yourself. They will provide more understanding of yourself and your tendencies.

How to Use Personality Assessments to Your Advantage

These tools are helpful for understanding yourself. Knowing your personality type can guide decisions on what will likely suit you or not suit your type. They undoubtedly have their role in your decision-making; they reveal your areas of strength and weakness. Also, they give you the confidence of your discovered purpose. Knowing your areas of weakness is good information. Your goal is to tap into your strengths and to improve your areas of weaknesses that are important to fully living your purpose.

> *Some of your areas of weakness may not affect living your purpose in any significant way. For example, a person who is highly aggressive will find this attribute useful in a career as a military officer or firefighter. If you don't have passion for any of these careers, rather, you want to be a social worker or nurse, for example, your exceptional ability to be sensitive (or empathetic) to people's feelings might be a strength for this career. Therefore, should your personality test reveal that you have low aggression, you don't have to try to become aggressive.*

- ❖ **Typically, how God has hard-wired you will often match with your authentic desires or passions. That is why it is important to listen to the voice inside you that is begging for expression.**

Let's look at the benefits of the personality assessments tests and the new tools as well as how to use the knowledge to our advantage.

Benefits of the personality tests: There is a place for using these important tools and knowledge about your personality. The assessment can confirm what you already FEEL/KNOW inside (i.e., instincts), which is far more honest or reliable than an external test. Apply them carefully. I recommend that you compare your APPP, Purpose Statement (PS) and DPP results with the results of the personality test you used. It will strengthen your understanding of yourself – tendencies, and other qualities. Also, personality tests can generally point you to career ideas.

Benefits of the three NEW TOOLS: The APPP, PS and DPP in this book reveal specific details that help you choose more accurately. The specific subject matters, issues, talents or gifts, potentials, passions and pains, and passions' impacts on you and others (from the discovery process), provide rich data. With this, you can make well-informed, accurate decisions about your specific purpose. Nonetheless, the personality assessment tests offer a general view of your tendencies.

Using the knowledge: It is obvious that practices that produce more accurate knowledge of one's purpose are essential. Young people in Western countries may have had formal conversations with a guidance or career counsellor during high school. Yet, many graduate from high school without a clear career in mind that allows them to be true to their purpose. Even in Christian schools, students may not be taught how to use their endowments within God's intended grand and specific purpose for their lives.

We must apply the knowledge and understanding we have found to improve our lives. King Solomon, the wisest (and richest) man who ever lived in the history of the Bible, encourages us to get wisdom and understanding.

> *"Blessed is the one who finds wisdom, and the one who gets understanding"* (Proverbs 3:13 ESV).

Also, he adds:

> *"Wisdom is the principal thing; Therefore, get wisdom. And in all your getting, get understanding* (Proverbs 4:7).

Why is there so much knowledge we haven't fully used for our improvement? Is lack of understanding the problem?

- ***God is the author or owner of every research, knowledge, and wisdom.***

For example, God allowed us to understand the personalities He created so that we can understand ourselves better.

Albert Einstein wrote, "***Any fool can know. The point is to understand.***" In other words, learn all you can to know, but *apply and adapt* the knowledge cautiously with understanding and your *understanding will grow* from the knowledge you applied.

In conclusion, we discussed important considerations when planning your education and training. But before that, using personality tests will provide a general view of your tendencies that can complement your more thorough and precise purpose discovery possible because of the APPP, PS and DPP tools. Here, I recommend that you use personality assessment tools and the new tools to achieve a greater understanding of your purpose. Also, we must understand that our relationships can determine whether we live our purpose. In the next chapter, I will examine courtship, marriage, and friendship decisions and how they must also be purpose-driven to maximize living your purpose.

Chapter 13

Making Relationship Decisions

We need people. God created us as relational beings who need one another. Your purpose does not fulfill you if others don't find value so that they help you. You need people to develop your purpose.

Whatever you do is enjoyable because it provides for others, and you're motivated that way:

- ✓ You're motivated to keep developing new products *for people.*
- ✓ You're motivated to embark on new research, new scientific discoveries, new technologies, new treatment protocols and new approaches *to help people.*

- ✓ You're motivated to design new clothes and to create new styles of dance, and new song rhythms with your instrument because *people* (will) *enjoy it.*

It is because you imagine how it will make others (PEOPLE) feel or you see how it benefits others (PEOPLE), who are motivated. PEOPLE motivate YOU.

> *We are made for one another; we are made to have relationships. A good marriage or friendship decision that supports your purpose gets you to the life that you desire. Everyone needs somebody. Someone builds you, guides you, inspires you, and nurtures you. You must be in a relationship with a person or persons who complement(s) you and make(s) room for you to flourish in your purpose.*

Often, being around or spending time with the wrong person(s) [not because they are bad people], who don't have what it takes to support building the potential in you can be frustrating. It can suck the joy and growth in your life.

Alternatively, you're on top of your life, receiving life into your purpose, when surrounded closely or even loosely by people who understand you. You're inspired to keep improving when these individuals know their role in your life and your role in theirs. In this chapter, I will discuss the importance of building the right relationships, including your romantic relationship and friendships. First, we consider courtship and marriage, and finally, friendship.

Courtship, Marriage and Your Purpose?

The direction in which you or another person are going can be an attraction to each other to become a couple. Sometimes, when two people take interest in each other, it is because of physical or emotional attraction only – that's being head over heels about your relationship. They follow mainly physical attraction or emotional compatibility (chemistry) with little to no reasoning on matters that are important to their life's purpose.

A reckless attitude to choosing a spouse is prevalent among the young and old. The results of an interview by Karl Pillemer, a gerontologist at Cornell University in New York, are quite revealing. He interviewed 1,500 seniors (65 years and over) who shared their regrets in life (Pawlowski, 2017).

The seniors said that they were not careful in choosing partners and that they perceived the relationship as a last chance. Could their hasty choices of partners be a result of desperation or strong emotions for the other without sufficient time to know the partner's reasoning, personality, values, attitudes, and life's purpose?

Serious Talk about Each Other's Purpose

Before a person decides to pursue a relationship, he or she must reflect on, at the very least, their abilities, potentials, passions, and pains (APPP). This reflection exercise is meant to guide the decision to choose the right compatible and supportive partner. People who are similar may like each other. But it is also true that opposites attract – meaning what you don't have, you may find attractive in someone else. The latter approach, in theory, can complete you when a person partnering with you possesses qualities that you desire. I say in 'natural terms' because only our relationship with God brings complete wholeness – both natural and spiritual wholeness.

When people are considering a potential life partner, they tend to focus on a general sense of each other's likes and dislikes. Beyond that is this:

- ***Have (discover) a clear sense of your own purpose and discuss it with your potential partner to ascertain if you will support each other in them.***

Sharing this knowledge of your purpose generates particularly important conversations that can determine whether you can be supportive of each other's purpose.

Assuming one is passionate about a career in music. A partner who has zero interest in being around music frequently can set serious mismatch issues, such as frustration and displeasure in their relationship. There is no concern when the two are willing to support each other even though it might not be 'his or her thing.'

Since career choice has a big impact on a relationship, you must know the extent to which you will love, accommodate, and support your partner's dreams or interests. I know of too many stories of couples who ended up calling it quits early in the relationship because they had far too different interests.

> *Dominique is an athlete and thus a public figure. He is always out with friends and to charity events that support child and youth projects for his community and internationally. Whereas Jaqueline is an introvert who loves running her childcare business at home, which allows her to homeschool their three sons – ages 11, 9 and 3. Jaqueline loves the comfort of her home and hates the glare and attention of the public. Dressing up to attend Christmas parties is not fun for her at all. Compromise is key in such a home.*

But if from the onset of the relationship all cards are laid on the table and you take time to understand each other's purpose, then this will help you to ensure he or she is the right one before committing to a life together. ***You can discover your purpose together using the tools in this book to enable you to make informed choices.*** Even friendships also benefit from knowing one another's purpose.

Where Do Friends Fit in Your Purpose

The saying that 'show me your friend and I show you your future' is undoubtedly true. Whoever you build a friendship with is a person you agree with.

<u>ONE or MORE of the following is true if you're friends with someone or certain people:</u>

- ✓ You like where they are going in life.
- ✓ You like their attitudes and position on various matters.
- ✓ You don't mind learning what they know.
- ✓ You like their taste or appetites (even if you don't have those same tastes).
- ✓ They can be your role models.
- ✓ You aspire to do some of the things you see them doing.

All these have big impact on who you become. This is the reason that you just don't make friends without reflecting on the lives of the people you wish to associate with, who may possibly influence you.

Make friends with those whose aspirations and values align with yours. The saying: "Iron sharpens iron" is true without a doubt. Suppose you wish to embark on a career in teaching, a purpose-focused person will build a relationship with other student teachers and those who have graduated and teaching or retired. These friends become your peers and mentors. If you're already teaching school, then, your school or institution colleagues or peers become your 'family' support and mentors.

Additionally, the teachers already working are crucial in motivating and guiding you. They are the people you will look to for encouragement when your studies and training become challenging. The mere fact that you're connected with a teacher-mentor, means this person can talk you out of discouragement or fears arising from the job. Similarly, with a retired teacher as a mentor, you will have guidance. They are also a source of inspiration.

However, if you choose friends (or mentors or coaches) whose values conflict with yours, you hinder and endanger your purpose.

You may even lose your soul (salvation) if this friend you look up to misleads you into a cult, false faith, or a reckless lifestyle.

Associate with wise, God-fearing, and prayerful people within those fields you aspire to be in, and you will become like them.

> *"Walk with the wise and become wise, for a companion of fools suffers harm"* (Proverbs 13: 20).

The opposite is true, too, if you choose the wrong circle of friends:

> "[24]*Do not make friends with a hot-tempered person, do not associate with one easily angered, [25]or you may learn their ways and get yourself ensnared"* (Proverbs 22: 24 -25).

This means that you must not be in toxic friendships. You must make friends with people who build you and you build them.

Build It: Friends Are Your Capital

Friendship is a form of social capital in which mutual support must exist. Having the right kinds of friends with values that you cherish builds you into the next phase of your growth. Your friends at different stages in life should contribute to building your purpose.

Be watchful when your friends become a danger to your purpose; you can't afford to keep such friendships. Separation is a good remedy at least temporarily. We saw how Joseph's dream of becoming a leader became a source of jealousy and hatred towards him. It was good that his brothers sold him away to a merchant who also sold him into slavery in Egypt. It was necessary for him to depart from them so that God will build his glorious future (in his series of dreams) out of the sight of his resentful brothers. Joseph reunited with his family when the time was right; when this slave boy had become the second in command in Egypt (Genesis 37: 18-38, Genesis 45-47).

<u>Losing those friends for a period can be painful, but it saves your life's purpose, therefore,</u>

- Dissociate from any toxic friends.
- Leave friends who retard your progress.
- Disconnect from friends who hate you or are jealous of you.

Moreover, you must shield your dream from well-meaning naysayers (friends and even family members), wishing you follow an average dream which they believe is possible for you. Like a hen over an egg incubating it, shield your dream for it to hatch before exposing it; this will safeguard you from being demotivated by their perceptions and utterances.

Also, choose friends with mutual interests in building each other. Elliott whined about his life. At the age of 30, he had moved from Cameroon to Dubai, felt stuck without a high school diploma and career at 38. Elliot had magnificent dreams since he was a teenager. His conversations always started with regrets for those wrong friends, and ended in great hope in God, that, he will one day live his dreams. He felt disappointed because his friends rejected him several times when he got into trouble with the law. You must build one another's purpose in friendship because your friend looks up to your help.

- ❖ Not only are you making friends with others, but you're also someone's friend. Someone looks up to you as a friend, mentor, and role model to guide and support his or her dreams.

- **How seriously are you taking your friendships?**
- **Are you being a positive influence on your friends' dreams?**
- **Are you motivating someone's purpose?**

Also, build mentoring relationships with others who are less skilled or mature to add value to their purpose and yours. What you give to someone you will receive in a larger amount (Luke 6:38). You learn from them as you share your skills, knowledge, money, and other resources with them. Everyone comes into your life with life experiences, skills, interests, dispositions, and potentials that are unlike yours. When you nurture their purpose, yours is nurtured, too, by the endowments they bring.

We have seen that since we are made to help one another, courtship, marriage, or friends must mutually benefit your individual purpose. A relationship in which goodwill towards each other's purpose doesn't exist is unnecessary. Besides, I encourage you to invest in a relationship with those disadvantaged with potential needing your mentoring. In the next chapter, I will present a concluding summary of the book, calling you to action to become your unique fulfilling self.

Chapter 14

Conclusion

Living by your purpose is living God's reason for your existence or your practical use. *As we have seen through this book, God instructs humanity – you and I – to be fruitful, multiply, replenish the earth and have dominion over all things He created – this is His grand purpose for us (Genesis 1:28).* Within this grand purpose, is your specific purpose (personal and unique to you) that you must discover and live so that you can occupy this prominent place of fruitfulness and dominion.

As pointed out, it is a tragedy that the children of God have been living below God's reason for their existence, because of a lack of practical knowledge to assist them to discover their purpose. This book is from my experiences and those of others, culminating into a strategic guide for your purpose-centred, fruitful and dominion life.

In this book, I talked about my concern over many youths and adults left confused, frustrated without a clear purpose. They draw from scenarios of several talented people who wallowed in long meanderings as if living a purposeful life is an illusion or false idea. But this is not so. I illustrated how distractions from family, friends, church, and other social networks, as well as early sexual experimentation and reckless living, hinder discovering and living our purpose. ***For you to live in your purpose, I called for distracting influences to be silenced, and holy living to be restored to prepare you to be all God intended you to be on earth.***

Further, I emphasized the key role of our imagination: our ability to see the possibilities in our mental imagery and in our spirits. I showed that everyone needs a powerful imagination that facilitates dreams to become physically real. I invited you to resurrect the force of your imagination given that some may have neglected it – you can only have what you see or imagine.

Further, the book demonstrated that what you need to grasp is how God hard-wired you for the purpose He has in mind for you so that you won't be a disappointment to Him, humanity and to yourself. It was clear that to live your purpose, you must discover it first. The secret is this: you must search or dig your purpose to unravel it.

Unravelling your purpose must be founded on an understanding of your divine connection with God. Therefore, I discussed God's grand purpose for humanity and key questions that you must answer to discover your specific purpose or practical use. Given that you belong to God, means you must live to honour Him because you will return to Him one day and account for how you lived. Moreover, I guided you on how to discover this specific reason for your existence, which you determine by how you're hardwired, expressed by the corresponding activities you will do in contributing to accomplishing God's grand purpose.

I have established that before you can live out your purpose, you must discover God's plan or blueprint for your life. This book has provided a step-by-step guide on how to discover that blueprint, which is your specific unique purpose.

To discover this purpose, I demonstrated the first step, a self-inquiry and assessment process, to unveil your assets or resources: abilities, potentials, passions, and pains, also your backbone (i.e., the APPP or AP^3). I pointed out that with the help of trusted others, you must deeply reflect and pray in this phase of discovery because precious 'minerals' (like your APPP) are only discovered deep in the ground;' in the depth of your spirit.

I illustrated how to use your four main resources, the APPP or AP^3, to create a Purpose Statement, from which you identify matching activities you will do, and create a picture representation called Detailed Picture Purpose – DPP. The creative picture representations provide an easy understanding of your purpose to you and others. And I cautioned that you must ***act*** on only activities with compelling reasons that improve lives. ***Plus, the simple activities presented help you to build hands-on experience as you follow, practice, and build mastery on this process of discovering your purpose.***

A discovered purpose is only beneficial if you use it to guide decisions and actions that support your purpose. I pointed out that key decisions such as career, education, training, and relationship decisions make or break your purpose. Therefore, I demonstrated how to use the DPP and others in making these important life decisions well.

I showed you how to choose your career and plan your education and training using the decision and planning tools I provided. Also, I noted the opportunity to complement the discovery process with the psychology-based personality testing tools.

Finally, I emphasized that relationships such as courtship, marriage, friendship and others must align with your specific purpose. Using various scenarios, I suggested what to expect in the right partner, spouse, friends and other relationships that nourish and support your purpose. As well, I cautioned the kinds of relationships to avoid, to see your purpose become a reality.

In a nutshell, this book gave you an outline as well as the nuts and bolts for discovering your purpose, and how to use your discovered purpose to live your satisfying, fruitful (prosperous) and dominion life that God intended for you. **What will you do with what you know now?**

Last Words: Dare to Step Up to Your Purpose

You have an opportunity to do something different if what you have been doing over the years has not worked well. To expect a different result from doing what you have always done is irrational. Today, tell yourself you're going to do something different. I did the same. I chose a new way because I got tired of living in the future and of making excuses.

No more excuses of why I couldn't do this or that.

- No more,' I'm not good enough.'
- Or 'I was raised in a single-family home, so I missed important emotional nurturing.'
- No more, 'my parents, church, schoolteachers, or counsellors didn't teach me how to discover and live my purpose.'
- Or 'I'm too old to get into this purpose talk.'

Who cares about your past, when you're new in Christ (2 Corinthians 5:17) when you're wiser and more empowered? <u>Today is a new day, it is a new opportunity;</u>

you have new knowledge, new insights to replace those not-so-good ones so that you can do what was previously impossible for you.

I needed to step up now, not later, so I did. I did this by writing this book. The journey has *challenges* but also *opportunities.* This mix keeps life interesting and non-stop while we live. Joyce Meyer said: postpone your fears for later until say Friday night (jokingly). Set up an appointment with yourself to deal with your fears on that Friday, and guess what? They won't be there come Friday night. By that later day, you would have moved on into unravelling and living your purpose.

Don't depend on someone's approval to start living your purpose. Respect people's opinions, but don't let them talk you out of your purpose. They were not there when God spoke to you. They were not there when you heard that inner voice saying, you can do well at singing, solving mathematical problems, plumbing, preaching, hairdressing, curing the sick or teaching? Ignore your naysayers and focus on your unique purpose.

Focus on your purpose, ignore distractions. In an interview on the local news station WPDE, a journalist asked Annie Mae Belin, a Darlington, South Carolina resident, who celebrated her 102nd birthday on June 1, 2021: *what is the secret to your long life?* She answered, ***"…. tend to [mind] my own business. And leave other people's business alone"*** is the secret (Brown, 2021, Interview with Annie Mae Belin).

I taught that was weird and so I laughed quietly. Then I pondered on what she meant; if minding your own business can give you long life, then what will happen if you focus on your own purpose? She is saying, leave out the excessive worry about what others think of you. Obsession with the lives of others or worrying about their perception of you is a distraction to your purpose. Your observers may be also trying to figure out their lives just as you are. Use them to encourage yourself. Therefore, keep your gaze on what you're doing – on your purpose.

Believe in God's capabilities and endowments in you. Believe in the exceptional value God has placed in you. Walk in wisdom and in the Holy Spirit, so that you don't miss out on what God is doing and will do in you.

> *"Then Jesus said, ……if you believe, you will see the glory of God?* (John 11:40).

So, believe! The *'glory'* (honour, blessing) in John 11:40 belongs to those who have made Jesus Christ the Lord of their lives, who love God and obey His word. You have an opportunity today to make Jesus Christ the Lord of your life, to be born-again, to become a follower of Christ so that God's word and the Holy Spirit will guide you in living your purpose.

To be born-again and become a follower of Jesus Christ, pray this after me:

> **"Dear Jesus, I make you the Lord of my life. I believe that you died on the cross for my sins. Forgive me of my sins. I promise to love you for the rest of my life. So, help me God...in Jesus' name. Amen!"**

✓ If you prayed this prayer sincerely, congratulations! You're now a new person in Christ. Heaven is rejoicing because your soul is recorded in the book of those slated for heaven. You're blessed!

Next steps:

- ✓ Get a Bible and start reading it. Ask the Holy Spirit to teach you and reveal Christ to you as you study.
- ✓ Find yourself a Bible-believing church to grow in your faith.
- ✓ For more resources to guide you, connect with Inspiring Purpose Academy *via* carku9@gmail.com

I pray that all you've learned in this book will take you to living your purpose. You're making it to the glory of God in Jesus' name. Amen!

If you have benefitted from this book, please recommend it to others. And don't forget to leave a positive review on the platform from which you purchased it. God bless you.

References

Bourdieu, P. (1986). The forms of capital. In J. C. Richardson (Ed.), *Handbook of theory and research in the sociology of education*. New York: Greenwood.

Brown, K. A. (2021, June 22). *A 102-year-old woman says the secret to longevity is minding your own business*. https://www.msn.com/en-us/news/us/102-year-old-darlington-woman-goes-viral-for-minding-her-own-business/ar-AALpuE4

Castrillon, C. (2021). *This is how highly successful people achieve career goals*. https://corporateescapeartist.com/this-is-how-highly-successful-people-achieve-career-goals/

Cho Y. D. (2020). *The fourth dimension. Discovering a new world of answered prayer. Special combined edition – Volumes one and two.* Reprint. Bridge Logos.

De Janasz, S., Dowd, K., & Schneider, B. (2021). *Interpersonal skills in organizations, 7th Edition.* McGraw Hill.

EducatingEngineers.com (2017). *Engineer careers list.* https://educatingengineers.com/career-specialties

Government of Ontario (2018). *Community mental health careers.* https://www.workinginmentalhealth.ca/forms/career.aspx#:~:text=Names%20like%20Medicine%20People%20or%20Shaman%20are%20sometimes,train%20for%20years%20by%20apprenticing%20with%20another%20Healer

Matthews, K. (2019, May 14). *8 Modern personality assessment tools for your HR team.* https://hrdailyadvisor.blr.com/2019/05/02/8-modern-personality-assessment-tools-for-your-hr-team/

Munroe, M. (n.d.). Collections of Dr. Myles Munroe. [Videos]. YouTube.

OECD (2014). *Glossary of statistic terms.* https://stats.oecd.org/glossary/detail.asp?ID=3560

Pawlowski, A. (2017, November 17). How to live life without major regrets: 8 lessons from older

Americans. *Today*. https://www.today.com/health/biggest-regrets-older-people-share-what-they-d-do-differently-t118918

Psychology Today (2021). Personality Tests. https://www.psychologytoday.com/us/basics/personality/personality-tests

True Colours (2021). *True colours*. https://truecolorsintl.com/what-is-true-colors/#:~:text=The%20colors%20of%20Orange%2C%20Gold,styles%20being%20the%20most%20dominant.&text=All%20of%20which%20testify%20to%20the%20benefits%20of%20True%20Colors

Manufactured by Amazon.ca
Bolton, ON

24896177R00146